On
Purpose
Before
Twenty

Boys of Few Words
Raising Our Sons to Communicate and Connect

~

No Mind Left Behind
*Understanding and Fostering Executive Control —
The Eight Essential Brain Skills Every Child Needs to Thrive*

On Purpose Before Twenty

Selected Essays

ADAM COX

FCP

Four Corners Press

· 2012 ·

FOUR CORNERS PRESS
Tiverton, Rhode Island

Contact the author: www.DrAdamCox.com

One of the essays in this collection, "The Case for Boredom," first appeared in *The New Atlantis.*

ISBN-10: 0985987901
ISBN-13: 978-0-9859879-0-9

LCCN: 2012948383

Library of Congress subject headings: Psychology — child; Psychology — adolescence; Parenting; Popular culture; Essays — 21st century

Designed and typeset by Joshua Langman
JL TYPOGRAPHIC DESIGN

This book is set in Linotype Janson Text, a type family designed by Hermann Zapf in 1954 and digitized by Adrian Frutiger in 1985. Janson Text is a revival of a type cut by Miklós Kis, circa 1685. The display type is Galahad, designed by Alan A. Blackman in 1994.

A man should not just work hard, but work hard for significant goals. JOHN ADAMS

[She] sees not the world before her but the one that is to be made, and the imaginative mind coupled with the prodigious strength of feeling becomes wedded to a single-mindedness of purpose that will not be weakened by complex or inappropriate emotions.
VIVIAN GORNICK, introduction to
Willa Cather's *O Pioneers!*

Our model citizen is a sophisticate who before puberty understands how to produce a baby, but who at the age of thirty will not know how to produce a potato.
WENDELL BERRY, *Think Little*

Every thinker puts some portion of an apparently stable world in peril, and no one can wholly predict what will emerge in its place. JOHN DEWEY

Contents

Preface

FOR AS LONG as writers have opined about youth they have been concerned with childhood's problems, more than its potential. Imagine a comparable literature of adulthood, one in which the main things discussed are what is a responsibility or a worry to others. New perspectives of cultural differences have not yet spurred an equivalent reorientation to *time of life*, particularly childhood. Although youth is the focus of frequent examination, our discoveries have traced the outward contours of their being — their care, training, education, and abilities. And while neuroscience has allowed us to peer into their physical brains, we've done far less to look within the psyche of youth. The essays collected here address that imbalance by telling a different story of youth. The basic idea is this: young people want an opportunity to participate in making the world, and are strengthened when their voices and capabilities are held in serious regard. It is through myriad forms of "making" that significance and purpose are discovered. This is youth's most important, and least told story. It is of immediate relevance to life between the ages of four and twenty, and to those who raise and teach the young.

Childhood evinces a sense of mystery that is the source of both its charm and concern. That secrecy is compelling, because it conceals the code of our beginnings. If you believe that being loved is what children want most, I ask you to reconsider. Love is certainly the foundation for all else, but in most cases, it is assumed and readily given. There is something else, however, less certain yet potentially life-changing — an opportunity to be significant, and to know the pleasures of purpose. As reflected in the title of this book, the theme of purpose weaves throughout these essays. Please don't be misled into thinking I am recommending a special, lofty status for a privileged few. These writings are not a recipe for self-absorption. Knowing a purpose is not elitism.

My thoughts about purpose pertain to an opportunity to do important things, and to be recognized for those contributions. I also mean the confidence and satisfaction that grows from self-discovery. Let me confess my belief at the outset that adults unknowingly obstruct this discovery among the young. Because children and adolescents depend on adults for basic needs, there is a reflexive tendency to think of them as not yet complete, as though personhood does not emerge until one becomes an adult. Yet at this moment, young minds are incubating, hopeful of making significant contributions to the world. This is not the *burden* of youth, it's what is exciting, and most interesting.

There is a place for pragmatism in considering the next generation. But we should not misinterpret this circumstance as a call to constrict, and thus falsify, our discussion of youth. That is the hurdle faced by those aspiring to illuminate a deeper story of childhood. Generally, if one writes about children, there is an expectation that the tone should be simple and reassuring — less literary than "useful." Editors advise: don't raise a problem for which there is no immediate answer, stick to practical suggestions, don't offend or worry any reader, be brief. The message here is that youth is a problem to be solved, and that the only thoughts worth having are those prompted by worry. This is an attitude at odds with the energy and optimism of youth, and a denial of our deep interest in the psychology of children. A review of those articles most widely read and shared by periodical and newspaper readers amply illustrates this fact. In my view, this interest is a notable dimension of our character — and we should embrace it.

The ideas put forth here were propelled by a unique opportunity to interview school age boys around the world about how they derive a sense of meaning and purpose from life. This was not an academic exercise; it involved days of intense, small group dialogue and listening in an attempt to glean what was significant. The conversations were serious and productive. What I learned during these conversations, and from my clinical work as a child and adolescent psychologist, informs these essays, and suggests a new set of coordinates for thinking about what makes a good life. These writings address both genders, and they concern young children as much as they do those finishing secondary school.

It is not my intention to convince you that childhood is important. I think you already know that. I would like to persuade you, however, that the spirit of youth has been left to drift. For most, there is an enormous gap between who they imagine themselves to be, and what their lives actually consist of. We should inquire: what is the work of children, and how does that relate to school? Why are we seeing a "failure to launch" among so many young men? How is the next generation radically different in terms of motivation, priorities, and communication? What is it that children most want from their parents, and need from their teachers? How does rebellion look different now? What is the hidden value of boredom? Why are K–12 schools more important than previously imagined to the resilience of societies and growth of economies?

A focus on purpose signals a change of course, emphasizing the potential of youth, more than its liabilities. The interests and capabilities of young people are ignored at peril. We risk truncating the momentum of individuals, and the wellbeing of societies; we foster recession rather than growth. The next generation is conveying its demand to be taken seriously through bold action, lifestyle choices, and disregard for what it sees as antiquated approaches to work and community life. Meeting this demand is not only ideal, but practical. Our regard for youth makes the world a more welcoming place; it is as much a form of essential stewardship as protecting forests, and creatures living on the brink of extinction. Providing spark for this dialogue is my own purpose, and what I hope is the significance of this book.

On
Purpose
Before
Twenty

The Purpose of Work

I

THE PRIMARY MISSING INGREDIENT in the lives of young people — the opportunity that separates them from a sense of personal accomplishment, maturity, and resilience — is purposeful work. This is not to say the young don't have work to do, because they are assigned plenty, but it's work that rarely ascends beyond academic assignments, family chores, and directionless retail labor. To accept this latter category and its perfunctory kin as the standard on-ramp for vocation is to confuse young people about what learning to work implies. And in fact, few adequately understand how profoundly work will come to occupy their lives, or the urgency of establishing an affirmative relationship with work — before they are pushed into a vocation at odds with their nature. I have spent two years talking with youth around the world about where they find significance in their lives, and my own sense of purpose in setting these words down has been ignited by what I have learned. Most important, I learned that attaining work which is a true vocation — a calling — is a more significant measure of happiness than any other event or opportunity that teenagers can imagine taking place in adulthood. This is not to say that the young don't have something to say about the merits of love. But when they are asked to reflect on the sort of happiness that is acquired by way of meaning and purpose, their unequivocal explanation for this effect is doing personally relevant, purposeful work. Although my recent research was limited to boys, owing to the interest of the project's sponsor,[1] I have no reason to believe that the imperative of finding purposeful work in life is any less relevant to girls. And in fact my conversations with girls, and visits to girls' schools, affirm that inclination.

Because *purposeful* work is virtually unrecognized as a critical source of meaning to young people, it is excluded from broader conversation about the emotional needs of the next generation. Worse, there is almost no dialogue about the need for purposeful work with young people themselves. Instead, work is confined to the more banal terms of job or career, effectively eliminating its relevance to personal industry, and one's prospective contribution to the world.

In suggesting that work can be purposeful, I refer to tasks that call someone to do something which is personally transformative. There is a good chance it will be work that is difficult to learn, because overcoming difficulty is partially where meaning and significance are drawn from. What separates this work from a job selected based on availability is that the task being done is connected with a personally relevant outcome. It is a mistake to assume such an aspiration is an entirely new phenomenon. In the eighteenth century John Adams advocated for "useful work," by which he meant work that was meaningful. According to historian Lisa Wilson, Adams meant that "a man should not just work hard, but work hard for significant goals... usefulness was industry with a distinguishable outcome."[2] The opportunity to act as an agent of achieving something tangible or important makes some types of work feel distinctly more purposeful. In the best cases, the concordance between work and worker is so great that the task being accomplished incorporates a palpable sense of authorship.

There are no specific restrictions on what type of work this might be, nor should there be any bias toward work that is inherently mental or physical. Working outdoors, in an office, alone or among others, are all equally eligible as prospective paths to purpose when the worker involved has a stake in the meaning of the work. If it seems unusual to be thinking of children and youth as the "worker" here, know that it is my intention to encourage this association. If work is thought of as only an encumbrance, we misunderstand its power to make life more interesting, and it is plainly wrong to exclude the young from these affirmative experiences.

It is easy to assume that the meaning of work is assigned based upon how plainly relevant the work is to life, or at least human life. By that standard, work that is literally a matter of life and death would sit atop the hierarchy of meaning, with other types of work having subordinate status. Thus an emergency room physician or military general would be thought to do very meaningful work. And of course this is true, but that understanding does not disqualify other types of work from being meaningful in their own right. I suspect most believe that work involving a high degree of craft is at least personally meaningful, and that work dedicated to improving the lives of others is also meaningful. The source of that meaning is both personal and contextual. If my work involves the pounding of nails, it will surely matter to me if I am pounding them into a cheaply made bookcase destined to sag, or if I am pounding them into a Habitat for Humanity home, knowing that my effort will result in something that will last for many years. In the latter case, there's ample visual evidence of my contribution, and a chance to know the people whose lives will be changed by my work. And although my contribution may not replace the need for compensation, it transcends the infantilization ingrained by most of the work offered to people under age twenty-five. That sort of work might aptly be called child labor, although there are no laws to protect the young from the emotional and intellectual vacuum of doing work with which they do not identify. We have a moral idea that one must start with unpleasant, boring, or degrading work and "earn" the right for more favorable terms. But is this the best way to introduce children to how absorbing work can be? Would we hand assembly manuals to kindergarten students, and allow stories only after they had proven themselves to be adept readers of technical instructions?

Purposeful work invites belief in one's right and responsibility to script his or her own life; to pursue work that is *ideal* because it is related to one's ideas about what is actually important to do. This is not the same as having a "dream job," a concept which disempowers almost everyone by suggesting good and satisfying work is as improbable and as unreal as a dream. To the contrary, good and purposeful work is grounded in reality, and is achieved not as the result of a dream but through choice and constructive action. Work fulfills these criteria only when the worker recognizes his or her right to feel identified with the outcome of the task. This sort of relationship is difficult, if not impossible, when work is done solely within organizations and hierarchies that lack flexibility, or demand a mindset of servitude. Purposeful work, and the weight of its life advantages, stems from a different set of criteria. Broadly understood, it is work that contributes to something of tangible, visible benefit, and which serves relevant human needs. The work may be principally mental or physical, but in either case it transcends the regressed idea of working *only* for pay: that equation is worse than servitude, it is economic enslavement. According to young people themselves, it is the single most ominous threat to adult happiness.

Meaningful work does not preclude compensation, but its meaning is in no way proportional to compensation. To conflate meaning and money is to dull an essential distinction that governs a hierarchy of work objectives. Just as all forms of work are potentially purposeful, every strata of the workforce has an opportunity to attain meaningful work. Purposeful is not exclusive to those with advanced degrees, or to the most intelligent and gifted members of society. It is the type of work which requires a period of reflection and experimentation, but which is accessible to all willing to seek it out.

If the idea and urgency of purposeful work strikes you as odd or confusing, then I'm concerned about your own history of work. The harsh reality is that many, if not most of us, have had insufficient opportunity to do purposeful work. It's therefore not surprising to find oneself at odds with the expenditure of energy required by work. Little experience is required to learn that work is not always pleasurable, and is often just the opposite. Work may be stressful, uncomfortable, and mentally taxing. Among younger people especially, *work may literally denote the opposite of pleasure, be viewed as obligatory, and experienced as a transgressive activity that infiltrates the boundaries of selfhood.* Adolescents learn to distract themselves while working as a means of decreasing their annoyance with having to do things that feel alien to who they imagine themselves to be. This way of working indicates an absence of purpose, and barely hides the melancholy work has caused. In such a psychology, work feels offensive in its audacity to interfere with psychic freedom and personal autonomy.

Deriving pleasure from work is untranslatable in lives where the least amount of interference from work is equated with the greatest personal victory. In taking flight from work, work itself is demonized, and hollowed of any meaning other than a way of getting to non-work pleasure. Work is perceived as a necessary compromise, a temporary surrender of spirit in exchange for the money needed to purchase whatever things and experiences are believed to actually make one happy. In this reduction, the good life is framed as maximized pleasure and amusement above all else. Such a conclusion would be radical if it weren't already so deeply entrenched in current cultural priorities. This includes the prolific production of games, and the belief that the more like a game life becomes, the less we will be burdened by boredom and the need to generate stimulation from within. This drastic life perspective effectively suffocates any alternative, and foreshadows an unsatisfying relationship with work. I write these words with grave concern that this conundrum already describes the nature of work for the majority.

II

Shifting attitudes about work, especially for youth, are part of broader changes in how we think and formulate priorities. What makes the current era unique is that our social and technological evolution has affected not only what we think about, but also how our brains work. Because of an acquired taste for constant stimulation, it is harder for most to sustain focused thought and self-awareness. It's an insidious tension that has slowly encroached upon our freedom by making it more difficult to step out of the passive consumption of stimulation, and into a more active role. The inertia of distraction and spectatorship has overwhelmed the momentum of living and doing. Yet this outcome has less to do with an epidemic of laziness than it does with the hypnotic fascination so many of us have with *watching*. A huge amount of life's content is accessed through electronic screens, and this tendency appears to affect young people without bias for education, gender, or socioeconomic status. Our preference for observing rather than doing, or to believe we *are* doing when we are actually watching, has become so reflexive that it may defy detection. When a habit becomes so commonplace that it feels natural, what is there to actually detect? Our inclination to watch points to a more fundamental reallocation of life than simply spending hours each day looking at screens. Specifically, our obsession with visual stimulation is testament to the increasing dominance of mind, and the power of electronic amusement to obstruct awareness of a larger sense of personhood and life purpose. A mind focused on its next stimulatory "fix" eventually devolves into an unproductive circularity that swirls counter to the momentum of purpose.

My intention is not to argue against the merits of using one's mind. But gluttony for cognitive stimulation inevitably minimizes life's prospective physicality. This is an enormous liability for the young whose first experiences with purposeful work are likely to include a physical component. The inherent abstractions of mind may cause us to drift deeper into a vortex of mirrors where all that we see — all that seems relevant — is a reflection of our mind-self. A never-ending loop of networked stimulation is captivating, but eventually makes life outside of such captivity seem dull, slow, and irrelevant. As communities become virtual, and virtually nothing more, connection within communities is organized primarily around sharing information. It is as if the posting of quips, media, or even "how to" information could be a suitable foundation for accomplishing important things together. Very little is tactile in the techno-mind labyrinth, although an engineer may soon make the apperception of texture a routine aspect of the computing experience. If so, this innovation will probably be heralded as ingenious. The basic sensory experiences of life will then be attained without having to move, and it will be as though simulated touch is sufficient consolation for never having a reason to leave our minds.

Little consideration is given to the bodily reflexes acquired through physical work, and the role those reflexes play in grounding the mind in a broader conception of personhood. I do not intend to deny the science of neurology, and what is proven about the chain of command between brain and limbs, but the conquest of mind is nearly complete when so many of us measure our happiness and self-worth according to the abilities of the mind. Our current condition prompts far-reaching questions about how life's meaning and the idea of happiness are changing. Is there a meaningful distinction to be made between being happy and being amused? Are we prepared to acknowledge that the ability to solve complex cognitive problems towers above all other abilities as the definition of what it means to be intelligent? Is it possible to deny our collective satisfaction with the physical distance of online communication? Embedded in such questions is an awareness that the body has gone underground. Beyond an imperative to maintain health and attraction, the body's productivity has become tangential to the good life. We should not be surprised. This is precisely the sort of servitude the mind demands.

III

Childhood and adolescence is a time of being pushed and pulled. These are distinct tensions that govern interaction between adults and children, and which require negotiation. Being pushed, even where it is warranted, generally feels unpleasant. Needing to be pushed suggests a person is not ready to move independently, and that contrived momentum is better than no momentum at all. By comparison, being pulled is more amiable, relying more on attraction than force. It feels more helpful than demanding, and more empathic than impatient. Practically speaking, we are likely to pull someone face to face, whereas pushing suggests a more anterior position. Someone can be pulled by another person, a situation, or valued opportunity. In contrast, we tend to be pushed around by obligations, deadlines, and a subordinate status. Unfortunately, work tends to inhabit our lives as a push more than a pull.

We are pushed to work when we are asked to do what is not of our own choosing, and when it is incongruent with who we feel ourselves to be. There is a difference between a task that is exceptionally difficult, but complementary to one's curiosity and ideals, and one that is difficult because it feels alien to a person's spirit. The former difficulty is the price we pay to do the work which calls us. The latter difficulty is never fully resolved; it is only tolerated and then briefly forgotten until it is time to do that work again. If this notion sounds like entitlement to you, then you might be among the chorus of those who condemn the lazy dreaminess of youth as a symptom of entitlement. To me, it is an earnest reaction toward a world indifferent to the distinction between work and labor, with labor being the sort of task most often assigned to youth, and which intentionally or not implies subordination.

To cite a common example, this distinction explains why young children are so much more eager to go to work *with* a parent than clean up their rooms. It is also a distinction that explains the onset of adolescent lethargy in the face of tasks that may be necessary, but are entirely uninteresting. Although labor is both necessary and useful, it is not a foundation upon which one builds identification with work. We generally do not feel "called" by labor, as compared with the interest inherent in doing purposeful work. A life that revolves around labor is primarily repetitive, and will require lots of pushing for things to be accomplished.

One reason few young people think favorably about work is because the spiritual affirmation of working is rarely discussed; it's hardly even relevant in places, including schools, where work is understood almost exclusively as a means to an end. Isn't it strange, or even alarming, that it's apparently unnatural for a parent or teacher to talk about how work grounds life in purpose? I suspect most adults have themselves been deprived of such discussion in their own upbringing, and would feel awkward initiating the topic with their offspring. In a difficult economy, that sort of discussion might even seem irrelevant, or audacious for the majority. Where does one get the moral authority to judge the goodness of work, when the attainment of any work is so elusive? The net effect is fear of raising basic questions about why we work, and what sorts of expectations we might bring to our work. This is not so much an economic conundrum as it is a loss of bearings. If none can agree where we are headed as a civilization, then of what consequence is it to measure the significance of our actions in the present? This ambivalence is symptomatic of a society in which many have lost pride in how time is allocated, and to what end.

My belief is that people of all ages, and young people more than others, are in immediate need of better education about work and vocation. Especially critical is helping children as young as six or seven to discover purpose through work. It takes time to sort out what one values and wants from life. As noted by psychologist Abraham Maslow, "It isn't normal to know what we want. It is a rare and difficult psychological achievement."[3] Opportunity for that discovery is abundant, however, if we will take the time to frame work as serious, and if we are inventive in balancing responsibility with autonomy. Younger children are thrilled to be charged with tasks that require them to make decisions, and to exercise good judgment. The learning requirements of work are what make it prospectively transcendent. I refer to work which means more than the immediate rewards it might produce. If a task does not hold the possibility of transcendence, then it is probably better understood as labor than work. The potential for transcendence is enhanced by doing work that draws upon one's abilities and interests. Some will dismiss these ideals as elitist or statistically improbable, but those arguments flow from a false understanding of how purpose is found.

I have a young neighbor who finds it intensely purposeful to fell trees with a chainsaw, and another who is on her way to a pet-care enterprise. These are the "dream" jobs of young people finding personal significance through work. And every such task necessarily enjoins distinct forms of intelligence. There is something admirable, and worthy of pride, in the ability to see a tangled forest and be able to differentiate trees that are healthy, old, valuable, or rare, and then know how to cut down the right ones safely and efficiently. Mistakes can be costly or deadly. There is something worthy in being responsible for a variety of animals as well — a majority of children understand this value intuitively. Good and purposeful work is not at odds with the demands of mind because it integrates the satisfaction of thinking and doing.

A basic juxtaposition to be noted here is that work can be either a source of attraction or repulsion. It is as fundamental a fact of life as love and death. When an attitude toward work has turned sickly or impoverished, it warrants the same serious concern we would give to a life-threatening disease. And in fact, we already act this way toward children who falter at school. As a society, we are generally agreed that an absence of synchrony with school has significant consequences, and we stand ready to intervene accordingly. Yet most forms of work go on for years beyond school, and play a more persistent role in shaping life satisfaction. The hunger for synchronous work is as deserving of our attention as those problems we refer to as learning disabilities. There is no difficulty finding a receptive audience for this dialogue among the young. Even the most minimal experience with work orients one to the urgency of the situation, and the desire to discuss it.

IV

The most disabling illusion about purposeful work is that it can be circumscribed as a specific kind of employment, or set of tasks. That perspective is unnecessarily limiting and obfuscates the central idea that work *becomes* purposeful when it is infused with spirit and intention. In this sense, purposeful work implies an emotive, focused disposition more than it does a system for assigning work value. Yet this principle does not imply that all tasks are equal in their purposefulness to different individuals. Some basic considerations need to be taken into account regarding an individual's core values, interests, and abilities. An assessment of those attributes guides the discovery of work that is congruent. However, trying to accomplish this assessment only through vocational tests is misguided, and may steer a person toward only the most conventional notions of career or work. It is better to expose young people to enthusiastic practitioners of varied vocational backgrounds, early in life, and to encourage discovery of what defines them.

By adolescence, the self has taken on a distinct form. Where the contours of this form are not detectable, it isn't because the self hasn't taken shape, it's because the attributes of selfhood have not been valued, discussed, and saved. Our life history is an atlas that defines who we are, and is an irreplaceable guide to where we might find purpose. It is unthinkable that we would never distill the wisdom and truth of this sort of self-knowledge. The logic underlying this mandate is that a life in which work nurtures one's nature is preferable to one in which work lies at the periphery of what is deemed to be important. In my own research, that need is voiced with certainty, and at least a little anxiety. Conducting interviews with several hundred boys of diverse backgrounds, in seven countries, I learned that their greatest anxiety about growing up is the possibility they will have to pursue work as adults that they do not enjoy. Probing the question further, I discovered that boys between the ages of nine and eighteen are worried that their future "career" might undermine rather than contribute to personal happiness. Their frequent reference to not wanting to be "stuck" encapsulates their dread of captivity by work done only for pay. The pressing nature of this angst prompts my own concern. I cannot ignore the anxiety encountered among these students, because it points toward a prescient intuition: a great many feel enslaved by work rather than activated by it. These same existential concerns about vocation are of paramount importance to girls, and deserve a spirited and thoughtful public dialogue.

Others have also observed the hub of concern surrounding vocation, and the disorientation that accompanies a disconnection with one's work. Michael Lerner, working with the Institute for Labor and Mental Health, in Oakland, California, investigated the concerns that affect people during a time of shifting political values. While he had expected to find that people were principally worried about protecting their assets, instead, he and others found a much deeper problem.

> On the contrary, we discovered that people were unhappy and unfulfilled, and what was striking as we delved into their pain was the similarity of their stories whose bottom line was: "I'm unhappy in the world of my work. I'm unhappy about what I do all day because I can't see what I'm doing as connecting to some meaningful life. I can't see how my work connects to any higher ethical or spiritual purpose. I can't see how I am serving the common good. I'm wasting my life."[4]

If a top-notch education is achieved as a hedge against economic uncertainty, the field of education, as a whole, has done much less to assert the relevant counterpoint: much of the happiness and meaning we want from life is grounded in doing good and purposeful work. Serious schools have long loathed the idea of being a job preparation program, because that idea seems to undermine the nobility of education. It's an almost correct defense against the historic and growing commercialization of education as "merely" the preparation of workers fit for the immediate needs of the economy. Emphasizing technical trades over the humanities is not my idea of helping students to find purposeful work. Studying the humanities enhances self-awareness, and may reinforce the purposefulness of work. Yet if the spirit of vocation is held at a distance, education can eliminate a principle source of meaning to students.

If the idea of being educated includes at least a nod to the importance of being a good citizen, then work must be a part of that equation. Work (by its productive and participatory nature) is a basic expression of citizenship for nearly everyone. Both work and citizenship have a common denominator in self-knowledge. This is knowledge that comes from creative work, important personal accomplishments, and critical experiences, all of which constitute an archive that should guide life planning. Yet for the most part, the possibility of life-affirming work is treated more like a lottery than the culmination of insight and thoughtful decision-making. The winners in this lottery will get work they adore, and a sense of being significant, and the rest will presumably soldier on as best they can. Most are asked to accept the idea that working at something personally irrelevant is a basic responsibility one cannot escape. Any emotional fallout from this contract is written off as growing pains, and resistance to "getting real" with life.

In my own psychotherapy with adults, work-related problems are discussed more often than sex, money, or childhood. Because work occupies so many waking hours, conflicts with work are ultimately significant life conflicts. It isn't uncommon to spend a dozen hours or more in therapy working out one's feelings about work. This is especially true of what might be termed *reactive work* — work that is done to meet basic needs, but which lacks the potential for personal resonance. We might agree that virtually all work has some purpose, but the radical humanist idea that the most formative aspects of work are its purpose and usefulness almost never surfaces in daily conversation. When lack of purposeful work does arise, it gets masked as a general malaise or discontentment with life. Remarkably, the relationship of work to depression barely warrants mention.

As a counterpoint, immersion in absorbing forms of industry suggests an approach to managing these anxieties. The self-control and accomplishment found in doing things purposefully is the great beginning of living a grounded, fulfilling life. Years ago, in the early years of my training as a psychologist, I completed a rotation on an adolescent psychiatric unit at Friends Hospital in Philadelphia. My task was to get hospitalized adolescents — some of whom were actively suicidal, and in one case, begging for electroconvulsive treatment — to attend group therapy. Making my rounds each morning, I would knock on doors, call out the patient's name and wait for a reply. Often, none came. Inquiring further, I would sometimes find young people crouched in corners, non-communicative and despondent. At first I didn't know what to do. The only things asked of these patients were that they attend to personal hygiene, and make their beds each day. Gradually, it occurred to me that this second task was an opportunity for them to gain some tangible control of life. This sounds absurd to everyone except, perhaps, those who have known the aimless lethargy of depression. And so I began to encourage and help with the making of beds, typically working in silence, but with a growing awareness that the care of the bed was a means of caring for oneself. Every second of attention and care invested in making a bed well stood in defiance of despondency's inertia; claiming the simple accomplishment of making a bed was a rung on the ladder out of depression. The application of care, which suggests the idea of doing something well, is the inverse of apathy.

For patients in a state of abject emptiness, those neatly made hospital beds became a measure of personal accomplishment, a sign that things were ever so slightly better. One shouldn't have to be hospitalized to be oriented to tasks that offer the possibility of transcendence, particularly when their earlier provision might have eliminated the need for hospitalization altogether. I do not believe in being glib with respect to a condition as serious as clinical depression, but the curative powers of work were well known to the Quaker founders of Friends Hospital centuries before more modern medical interventions. Providing patients with an opportunity to do meaningful work was part of what was termed "moral treatment" by psychiatry's earliest pioneers, because such work became a tangible bridge between illness and health; it was a promise of inclusion, and a means of anchoring purpose even in the throes of despair. Purposeful work is capable of shifting the psyche from a state of dependence and reactivity to self-control and autonomy. It is an opportunity that most young people subconsciously crave, but to which very few have access.

V

Although all work might be thought of as inherently purposeful, there is a difference between work that is pragmatically purposeful because it accomplishes its intended outcome, and work that *becomes* purposeful as an agent of personal transformation. In the latter case, work still needs to be directed toward a desirable outcome, but it achieves more than this — it reinforces a *constructive* relationship between thinking and doing. By illuminating this relationship it combats inertia, and is a counterpoint to the existential apathy so often misinterpreted as laziness.

Especially useful is work's ability to build self-knowledge through experimentation with different ways of being purposeful. Although each venture into purposefulness is necessarily limited by the parameters of the task or objective at hand, the accumulated effect of these experiences constitutes an enormous mental leap. Still, the purposeful work void for most youth does not deter expectation that their maturity will appear on schedule. It is as though we believe that the leap to adulthood can be accomplished through discipline and identification with adult values alone. But where is the opportunity to author one's own life? The time to begin practicing how to be an adult is before adulthood starts. The excitement of tuning in to one's calling is more absorbing than watching a screen. Emphasizing how work enhances the meaning of life is not merely a call for a change of social focus. It is recognition that the need for purpose arrives early in life when the impulse to industry is driven by vigor, and enthusiasm for helping to make the world. Very young children wake up excited to be *doing*. This is the natural human condition, and schools can — and should — build on that momentum from preschool through secondary education.

Purposeful work is transcendent because its net effect is more than the sum of its parts. It changes the doer of the work because it connects personal effort with a larger context of relevant communities. This is one basic way in which communities are built. Without opportunity to tangibly connect with others, community is little more than a noble idea. Consoling ourselves with thoughts of burgeoning *online communities* obfuscates the broader needs of living beings. Most of us, especially in youth, need some opportunity to do good and admirable work. That doesn't mean purpose is only found in tasks traditionally thought of as wholesome or pure. Such intuitions are anchored by distortion and sentimentality. Aiming to start a profitable business is no less purposeful than the will to build an animal shelter. Clinging to preconceptions about where and how purpose should be found potentially denies youth the right to construct purpose according to their own script.

In mid-life I find myself seriously and surprisingly dedicated to farming blueberries on a small parcel of sloped, rocky land. It's a project that has exhausted nearly all of my physical energy, and required me to partially neglect the professional work that has long been the basis of my living and whatever social status I might have earned. I am more reliant on aspirin than I ever wanted to be, and live in constant fear that hungry pests will devour years of work in one summer. Still, I recommend this sort of undertaking, if not the exact vocation. These days there are plenty of books that advocate an agrarian lifestyle and its many soulful pleasures. Although I'm an avid reader of these books, I have no expectation that this lifestyle will appeal to others, but it certainly might. Purpose is not found in a prescribed set of tasks, but in the meaning a task has for a specific individual. It is the feeling of having cultivated an authentic work identity which makes the doing of that work significant.

VI

Talking with young people about the origins of significance in their lives, I have found that most can comfortably converse about the possibility of *personal significance*. More often than not, they define personal significance as good character, like having integrity and being dedicated. In contrast, the attainment of *social significance* is viewed more as a matter of circumstance, or luck. So, being significant to a larger world is essentially viewed as outside of personal control. But why should such a mindset prevail in a world seemingly overwhelmed by the need for difference-makers? The cultural inclinations of North Americans, for example, prompts people to search for exceptionalism in the form of unscripted sacrifice, genius, or accomplishment. Those types of exceptionalism clearly stand on their own merits — yet does the "exceptional" always have to be rare and unassisted? Is that a wise strategy in a world whose most valuable resource is its people?

And why should exceptionalism have to emerge spontaneously for it to be valued? If the 20th century cultivated belief in iconoclastic geniuses, then here in the 21st century we need a narrative of more collaborative problem-solving, informed by the understanding that some coveted talents can only be realized through a network of gifted mentors and teachers. This perspective would expand the terms of exceptionalism to include those whose exceptional contribution is contingent upon support and affection.

It's no secret that human accomplishment tends to rise and fall with overt and covert expectations. In a classroom, for example, the expectations projected by a teacher usually influence student performance.[5] The outcome of the equation rests on the plausibility of a teacher's belief in a particular individual's potential. Deciding to believe in someone is not a publicity campaign employed to disguise grave doubt. It is more fundamentally a decision to suspend preconceptions about how well a person can do, and what form that person's accomplishments might assume. Cultivating an atmosphere of seriousness is the difference between merely expressing confidence in someone, and allowing oneself to believe that exceptional achievement is actually possible. It relies upon lopsided bias of unconditional belief — a determination to look past obstacles toward what might be possible.

One reason that the idea of work as a source of personal significance rarely takes root in younger people is that few believe their efforts as workers will be taken seriously. They are, with few exceptions, absolutely right; most of the work young people do is effectively reduced to an indication of compliance or good behavior. Compliance signals a promise that the moral fiber of a young person is intact, and that one is ready to take orders as adulthood begins. The limitations of this perspective are a serious obstacle to maturity. A younger person's need to participate in making the world *now* may go unconsidered. By making I mean *an opportunity to shape the world according to one's ideals; to address the tension between public and private narratives about what one should do.*

Given the amount of schoolwork and busywork assigned to children, and the over-scheduling and structure of children's activities, there has naturally been some pushback. We now have advocates for a childhood free of responsibility. But it is a mistake to resist any proposal for how children might be more *meaningfully* productive. This type of productivity is fundamental to their sense of inclusion and happiness. Advocacy for the freedom of childhood asserts the need to protect children from the sorts of external pressures that now encumber their lives. In my view, this critique has had the right concern but the wrong response. Certainly, children do not need three hours of homework and several résumé building activities each day. These activities are not authentic. But such righteous resistance has had the unfortunate effect of stifling relevant conversation about the value of purposeful work. It is perhaps not surprising that a society as self-absorbed as our own would so zealously protect an activity as solipsistic as play. This is not a criticism of play, or an assertion that its importance should be diminished. The cognitive and emotional advantages of play are well established. Yet there is a difference between how a child plays, and how that same child might also be guided toward self-revealing work.

Where play provides an opportunity for the dramatic projection of fantasies and conflict, work is accountable to human, animal and environmental needs. Thus work is inherently social, even when it is done alone. Young children play with the idea of accountability and purposefulness when they pretend to be someone with special abilities or powers. It is when projection transitions from role-play to watching television that the authorship of children is diminished. Then, the script is defined by others, and doing occurs only in the mind. (Although video games have incorporated role-play, the available roles are mostly preset. These games may involve intense amounts of stimulation, but allow minimal creativity, unless we are fooled into thinking that choosing the costume, weapons, or vehicle of a video character is what creativity now means.)

Play occupies life before work does, and is in ways a primer for work. As cleverly observed by philosopher Alain de Botton, children gravitate toward characters who are "shopkeepers, builders, cooks or farmers — *people whose labor can easily be linked to the visible betterment of human life.*"[6] In this way, children's books help facilitate the conversion of playfulness into industry that can be observed and practically measured. As the prospective roles of adulthood come into sharper focus, the ideals of young people often hover over work that is expressive, and which results in a visible and admirable outcome. Most young people are eager for admiration, and receiving it is a key source of compensation for working in the first place.

VII

An important reason that communities traditionally accept responsibility for teaching the young how to work is a common appreciation of how work fosters maturity. The avoidance of this responsibility achieves exactly the opposite result. By not teaching the young *how* to work we effectively stunt their maturity. Without the gravity that work affords a developing life, all emphasis is placed on school performance. School is then unnecessarily stripped of importance, because going to school needs to be infused by a spirit of vocation — being called to accomplish significant things. Sitting still in classrooms no longer has the relevance it once *seemed* to have. It's just not sensible to cultivate purpose in a learning context which is decidedly hands-off. Philosopher turned mechanic Matthew Crawford writes in *Shop Class as Soulcraft*, "In schools we create artificial learning environments for our children that they know to be contrived and undeserving of their full attention and engagement."[7] By artificial, Crawford is alluding to an environment without a hands-on opportunity to learn, but there is also the critical problem of the distance between learning and outcome. It simply takes too long to get an opportunity to apply what has been learned in the classroom. The preparation of young people goes on for many more years than most can tolerate. Why should one have to be in their mid-twenties before having a viable opportunity to gain and demonstrate some form of socially relevant competence?

In my view, and according to my own research, school would benefit from a sense of real-time urgency and necessity. Although adulthood is driven by all sorts of urgency and necessity, we are generally intent on protecting the young from the same. This is done with good intentions, yet once people reach adolescence, a denial of life's urgency reinforces magical thinking, and delays the onset of maturity. Much is written about the importance of encouraging attributes such as altruism and empathy, but how well do we understand the obstacles to these ideals? Where there is resistance, we might believe that altruism is anathema to youth itself, instead of seeing that altruism has its conditions.

A concise example of this phenomenon emerged when I asked students how many of them would be seriously interested in an activity or career that was focused on helping others. Approximately twenty percent of the boys I interviewed endorsed this idea. But having spent parts of two days talking with different students, I suspected that a much greater percentage would actually be interested in altruistic work if the conditions were right. Following that intuition, I formulated the following scenario and question: "Suppose that the head of your school walked into this meeting with a look of serious and immediate concern. And suppose he or she said that a call had just come in from the Mayor regarding an emergency in the city center, requesting that five students be recruited to assist the city with this urgent situation. And if your school head further stated that you will be expected to work until midnight, that you should expect to get filthy, possibly ruining your clothes, and that you will likely be exposed to foul language and the potential for danger, and that although you will be expected to give of your effort and focus completely, you are also expected to be cleaned up and ready for school on time tomorrow morning, how many of you would volunteer?" Can you imagine how this form of altruism affected the interest and emotions of boys in my study? Should it surprise us that nearly every student wants to volunteer for such an activity? It doesn't surprise me, and I believe that if we are willing to look objectively at the motives and ideals of young people, we will detect how *urgency* and *necessity* infuse work with meaning, making such experiences irresistible and indispensable.

VIII

There are some who might propose that where work and youth are concerned, the principal goal is to build character and a positive work ethic. This is certainly the prevailing philosophy in this part of New England where I learned to work as a boy, and now practice my profession. Although we might reasonably hope that character is in fact an outcome of good work, making character the objective of work undermines its potential resonance. The notion of building someone else's character, though it may be prompted by good intentions and high hopes, is fundamentally a push, and not a pull. It almost always involves the projection of one person's ideals onto another person. When work is done cooperatively with other people, there is an expectation of good conduct — a solid effort and positive attitude — even if it is unspoken. Problems emerge in cases where the expectation of good conduct is understood as the complete subordination of one's selfhood. That is why many entry-level jobs deflate the hopes of new workers. These types of parameters are commonly found in large corporations or perhaps in retail businesses that require compliance with scripted conduct, no matter what the circumstance. It is, for example, unreasonable to ask young people to adopt repressive standards of work conduct, and simultaneously ask them to consider their work as an extension of themselves.

In order for young people to embrace work in the way I am advocating, we will need to develop places and methods of working in which individuals are as important as the organizations they serve. While the steps to individual and organizational "success" may share superficial similarities, their ecologies are radically different. Communities that view the wellbeing of individuals as the essence of their strength act differently than those which perceive strength as a dominant stronghold of goods or services. In the latter formulation, the purpose of individuals is to maximize profit, which necessarily involves the suppression of personhood. Those students or workers who falter in this suppression threaten to undo productivity, and are thus dispensable. Business mogul and former CEO of General Electric, Jack Welch, is publicly applauded for taking dramatic action to sever those people who are perceived as giving too little to their employers. Under Welch, in a process sometimes referred to as "rank and yank," General Electric fired over one hundred thousand people by successively culling the bottom ten percent of performers.[8] It is surely no wonder many young people would prefer to fantasize about being rock stars, or become basement-dwelling gamers.

It is an unfortunate reality that most young people are oriented to work under the tutelage of someone who is a manager rather than a mentor. Consider the advice dispensed to would-be managers in *Managing for Dummies*. I understand that books such as these are written primarily for novices, but an argument could be made that most people are in fact being managed by novices, whose only understanding of management has been derived from manuals like *Managing for Dummies*. The psychological indoctrination of books like these plays upon the novice manager's fantasies of power and specialness. It is as if being welcomed into the management class conferred superhuman properties and special wisdom that workers themselves could not understand. For example, *Managing for Dummies* (more literal than humorous) urges managers to assess how their "workforce" (an inherently industrial term that pompously subordinates individual identities) perceives the "mission and purpose of the organization."[9] *Managing for Dummies* makes no apology for overlooking any possible purpose of individual workers, because that is not the concern of management. The personal needs of workers attract attention only when they threaten organizational profit.

Of course such corporations do not publicly denounce individual needs, because that is less defensible than framing purpose as an exclusively organizational theme. In having a "mission," it is possible to seem high-minded and noble, rather than mercenary. Indeed optimism itself is to be used as a means to boost productivity. The authors of *Managing for Dummies* note that "great leaders always see the future as a wonderful place." The explanation for this phenomenon is that "people want to feel good about themselves and their futures, and they want to work for winners." "Before long, a great leader can turn an organization full of naysayers into one that's overflowing with positive excitement for the future." The coercive megalomania of this approach is self evident, yet it's an approach that is undoubtedly applied in numerous organizations every day. I believe the young have been inoculated against empty rhetoric. We are raising a generation that has been exposed to what some estimate as five thousand ads per day, and which has adopted irony and cynicism as a defense against such dishonesty. Most feel too inexperienced and disempowered to challenge the absurdity outright. But they do know how to tune out.

The situation makes it abundantly clear how important purposeful work is to freedom of thought. Yet there is a giant gap between our cultural appreciation of political freedom, and freedom of mind. Americans, in particular, spend hours watching pundits debate shifting political freedoms, but give relatively little consideration to how difficult it has become to think outside of the staid parameters of our work lives. We use television ratings to interpret which ideology is winning the battle for public influence, when the true victors in this battle are those that command our attention so thoroughly that political and market narratives become more important than those that define our immediate lives. As managers of families and schools, we cannot afford to adopt the disguised selfishness of purpose demonstrated by market and media "cultures." We need an enlightened perspective of the relationship between work and conduct that addresses the need to pull the young toward what is naturally reinforcing, rather than pushing them toward the type of oppressive employment situations which diminish their capacity for mental freedom: the right to think for themselves.

When business books turn their attention to the priorities of individuals rather than those of organizations, advice is dispensed about how to get the most money for the least amount of work. Indeed, in many ways this is the guiding principle of post-industrial economies, and why those who never "game the system" effectively end up feeling resentful about having to work at all. The emptiness of this ethos is unconsciously articulated in a wide variety of books, but has rarely been advocated more succinctly than in the bestselling *The 4-Hour Workweek*, by Timothy Ferriss. I suspect that Mr. Ferriss is a decent individual who aspires to relieve people of the burden of working, which he understands to be drudgery. It seems unlikely he has ever perceived his work as purposeful beyond making enough money to do less work. At least in this book, Mr. Ferriss promises a lifestyle in which people will be able to allocate far more time to pleasure than work, and he outlines a whole host of strategies for attaining this objective. These strategies are described in the book's introduction as the prevailing practices of the "new rich," and it is suggested that they be emulated by those who themselves want to become newly rich. For the most part, the recommended strategies assume that one can cleverly take advantage of various economic subsystems, such as advertising or electronic communication, to make heaps of quick money.

The unembarrassed premise of these strategies is that *all* business is artifice, and that the sooner one accepts this fact, and figures out how to game the subsystems that generate business, the closer one is to "success." According to this ideal, success involves special privileges like playing golf in Aruba, or enjoying luxurious layovers in Dubai, rather than wasting one's time working. Ferriss astutely points out that our era celebrates the cult of the expert, and he asserts that expertise is a matter of clever positioning, rather than something earned by way of something as presumably banal as experience. "It's time to obliterate the cult of the expert," Ferris explains, "First and foremost, there is a difference between *being perceived* as an expert and *being one*. In the context of business, the former is what sells product and the latter ... is what creates good products and prevents returns."[10] Well, at least genuine expertise counts for something, even if it is not the main thing. Ferris goes on to explain the simple, non time-consuming steps to distort public perception so that one can be perceived as an expert as quickly and effortlessly as possible.

The 4-Hour Workweek was translated into thirty-five languages and no doubt devoured by an international readership no longer able to discern its inherent absurdities. It's also possible that few care about such distinctions, as long as they only have to work four hours per week. The question that has already vexed me for more than one of Mr. Ferriss's work weeks, however, is how consumers of his ideas can rationally be charged with the responsibility of orienting the next generation to the meaning of work? The Timothy Ferriss economy espouses economic freedom for anyone with the gumption to take it; greed and deception are not something to be moralized about, they are nuisances to be cleverly played because the point of life is to cram as much fun and indulgence as one possibly can into every moment.

The ugly secret hidden behind this view is that those who game their way to the top must trample on someone to get there. There is an assumption in such books that if you are smart enough to be reading the text, then you are more likely to be a trampler than the trampled. But the artifice of these books is so massive and audacious that it's hard to see that you have joined the community of the trampled the moment you give your money to the evangelist who promises you something for nothing. The most successful books of this genre will exceed all expectations, cutting their authors' four-hour work weeks in half, while leaving the rest of us in a dissociative funk about how we came up short, and feeling angry about having to work at all.

IX

Although my emphasis here has been the relevance of purposeful work for young people, there is no reason to believe work should be any less meaningful to older workers. The need for purpose does not disappear so much as it is gradually compartmentalized, and excluded from the expectations one holds for work. The imperative to provide opportunities for *purposeful work* lies in the belief that work can be an affirmative, defining experience. Young people need a chance to do work that is consistent with their interests and core values; something that will yield pride and self-directedness rather than a directionless, half-hearted effort. The latter is what many pessimistically hold to be the truth of work, and what we believe they must accept to be gainfully employed.

The most formative challenge in preparing the next generation to do purposeful work may be building their faith in its value. There is no better place to nurture this capacity than within a relationship of uncompromised hope between adult and child. In the simplest terms: *ideal work* is first imagined and desired for a child by the *ideal parent* or *ideal teacher*. In this way, the hope for a child to have good and purposeful work is an expression of unconditional positive regard. That regard suggests that a person is worthy of such autonomy, self-expression, and responsibility. This is not a mandate that parents or teachers secure such work for children. But it is an assertion that good work comes into a person's life through a belief that it can be an elevating human experience, and that all human beings are worthy of that possibility.

This is a sensitive point, and a juncture at which some might feel as though I am encouraging a sense of entitlement. Some contemporary parenting literature admonishes us for what is widely held to be an epidemic of entitlement, for teaching young people that they can have, and deserve, "it all." I do not disagree that such teaching goes on within some families, whether implicitly or explicitly. But to conclude that young people's ambivalence about work is principally because of what has been implied in families is to grossly underestimate the intelligence and sensitivity of the next generation. What surfaces as entitlement is a longing for more from life than what is currently offered. At the same time, I believe the young are unsure of what that something is, and where to find it.

The wound of disenfranchisement, inflicted by those who size you up and see no promise, is enormous and disabling. These are the invisible disabilities affecting those who sustain surface function. They follow rules, attend school, and get along well enough to avoid offense. Yet the lack of belief invested in them makes their lives unnecessarily hollow, and their momentum is in constant peril. And let us understand that many forms of so-called juvenile delinquency are essentially an intention to resist identification with social attitudes that ostracize those who do not readily conform. I find it difficult to be unsympathetic with the disenfranchised, and increasingly unsavory to align myself with those who ignore the formative contribution of meaningful work to being a citizen with a stake in this society.

Because I am a psychologist, it may not be surprising that I have focused my argument on the contribution of work to personhood — the capacity of work to expand a person's sense of meaning and satisfaction with life. Contrary to the cynical advice promulgated by business authors and their motivational speaking kin, I do not view work, mine or anyone else's, as deriving its meaning from the capacity to build wealth. It is true that in the best circumstances work builds an economy which serves the collective good by giving each of us a chance for a vocation of sufficient compensation. It is this dimension of the national economy which is most in need of rescue. Agrarian philosopher Wendell Berry has opined, "Among the many costs of the total economy, the loss of the principle of vocation is probably the most symptomatic and, from a cultural standpoint, the most critical. It is by the replacement of vocation with economic determinism that the exterior workings of a total economy destroy human character and culture also from the inside."

One might assume that these thoughts have little relevance in a time of economic crisis. But that conclusion lacks consideration of how the diminishment of vocation has made our desperation even more desperate. If part of the recession has been brought upon us by making unaffordable purchases, we must also realize that such transactions are made as emotional compensation for the loss of something more personal. The momentum of purposeful work is a renewable reservoir of energy and resilience, but it requires an orientation to both the seriousness of work, and life itself. That such a call to action has to be made signifies how far we have drifted as a civilization. How long it might take us to recover from this existential malady is hard to say. We can agree, I hope, that the way out of this cave and into the light of a more rational relationship with work is propelled by activating the latent purpose that animates every young life.

Sovereign Minds

IF UNEMPLOYMENT and a dearth of credit are the nemeses of the current economy, the next economy seems vulnerable to a different roadblock — a generational shift in what the "good life" actually means. It may turn out that lack of opportunity is less relevant to long-term growth than declining interest in one traditional denominator of a strong economy: job-first, work-for-pay lifestyles. Basically, the next generation shows few signs of wanting to work just because that's what people are supposed to do. This is a generation for whom "supposed to" is an emotional non-sequitur. It doesn't easily mesh with a life oriented toward personal preferences, speed, and a divorce from the sort of guilt that has traditionally underpinned the emotional life of workers.

Rising debt and the disappearance of jobs have led us to agonize about the young and unemployed, worrying that the next generation won't be able to work its way into the economy. But many young people seem to have circumvented that worry by rejecting the very thing that middle class culture is working so hard to preserve. It's not that young people don't want money, or think they can live without it, but there is increasing resistance to making work the focal point of life. Shifting generational priorities are in part triggered by less opportunity, but the more potent catalyst of this shift is the *neuro-social transformation* of adolescent values. As a child and adolescent psychologist, I've had a front row seat for this revolution, and it has been an object lesson in the reciprocal influence of mind and culture. In some respects, the next generation has acted powerfully to define itself, including its own work values. In other respects, such as the pervasive effects of culture on tempo and attention, the next generation has been profoundly influenced.

There is a declaration of psychological independence rising among the emergent generation, symbolic of a deep divide between 20th and 21st century ideals. It's a seismic shift in perspective more relevant to the economy than immigration policy, health insurance law, or the reconstruction of credit. This generational assertion of freedom includes the right to ignore the complex, impersonal schemes that have traditionally supported the gross national product. The millennials, like all generations, is comprised of at least a few subcultures. A part of this generation has moved forward into traditional workplaces, and is shaping the economy from within. My own attention, however, is drawn to a different sort of millennial — one who resists entering the workplace at all, or who insists upon a radically different orientation to work. Within the mind of this millennial, the idea of work is to serve the needs and *interests* of individuals. It is an attitude cast as entitlement by older generations, but felt very differently by young people themselves. It's also an outlook that is the pulse of what's called "failure to launch," although "failure" is a misnomer given the intentionality of this revolution.

This rebellion of ideals portends a change in the basic premises of a successful life. Practical reality, as conventionally understood, has little resonance for many millennials. And many older people have missed the turn made by this emboldened edge of youth. Our fundamental mistake in trying to "save" the coming generation is to assume they want to be just like us. They do not. The nub of this generational shift in vocational perspective has to do with a collision between evolving minds and socioeconomic circumstances. More specifically, *the next generation is making work subordinate to the tone and tempo of mind.* Work that does not appeal to the preferences of mind is not only unattractive, it fails to be morally persuasive. The best educated members of the next generation — those who have some power of choice — are unlikely to allow themselves to be employed by activities that feel alien to the new tempo of mind. The sway of this resistance is driven by a generational reflex to decide for oneself where and how to focus. Specifically, this is a generation which does not feel obligated to think or care about things which it finds personally irrelevant. It's post-ADHD. What appears to be disorder to those in midlife is the new normal for those under twenty-five. From the perch of adolescence, the real disorder lies in outdated systems of thinking and working, like the idea that people are obligated to force themselves to do work that they do not like. Given such an attitude, is it even reasonable to entertain the notion of large scale manufacturing re-emerging? Who among the next generation would perform such jobs? That way of working — subordinating one's own needs and ideals to a vertical command hierarchy — is as alien to the next generation as the formality of addressing someone as Mr. or Ms. This is a rapidly growing sensibility, fueled by a confident vision of a more horizontal world. And why not? Millennials have had a lifetime of exposure to the pre-ternaturally young and beautiful — depicted in positions of authority and creativity. In thirty years, our progeny may wonder why we, of the "Boomer" generation, were so willing to consign ourselves to an agenda of upward mobility. Where was our self-esteem?

A Problem of Inspiration

The credo of personal responsibility is a celebrated myth of American life, and sets the tone for how many parents relate to their children. At some point, every adolescent inspires a basic question: how close is this person to assuming responsibility for his or her own life? It's a concern that prompts us to motivate those whose lives seem stalled, or those who resist responsibility. We may believe that stalled momentum cries out for inspiration and direction. Yet the chink in our thinking is this: true motivation is never inspired. A majority of the young are predisposed to cast a wary eye toward anyone who seeks to orchestrate their will. No matter how it might be intended, an attempt at motivation is ultimately a desire to co-opt someone else's personal priorities. It is unavoidably contentious because it pits one person's will against another's.

It's easier to appreciate the necessity of motivation in thinking about activities like military service or sports, contexts where vigorous compliance is essential to victory. But motivating someone to "grow up" is considerably more complicated. Adults and adolescents don't necessarily agree on what merits effort, or what being "grown up" looks like. This dilemma underscores how supremely difficult it is to make someone want what they don't already desire. But is this really a problem, or simply a testament to human resilience? And could this resistance even be a prized aspect of identity, or political ideals? For example, how can we rationalize celebrating a cultural ethos of freedom, and then look askance at an individual's assertion of autonomy — even if that reflex is exercised in the interest of remaining idle, or what we consider to be "underachieving?"

Although the urge to think freely is a hallmark of adolescence, this expectation has historically been related to the *content* of thought, rather than its *form*. More precisely, adult culture has generally recognized the right to let one's mind drift toward what attracts it, but has been less tolerant of the pace and tangents of adolescent thought. Consequently, we get annoyed with young people who appear to be distracted, and especially with those whose mental effort seems lax, or indifferent to what we think is important.

This sort of impatience may have increasingly little

effect, however, because the newest forms of mental freedom have different roots, and a new look. The implosion of knowledge hierarchies is signified by the information mashups of online culture. A hallmark of these mashups is the decentralization of knowledge; what is held to be true or real is more malleable. Even the most trusted voices must compete for influence among others who are tweeting at the speed of thought. Following this trend, there is an impulse toward thinking temporally; a tendency to build one's truth from a pastiche of content that approximates collage. The very concept of authorship (and by extension, ownership) is being rigorously challenged. Who owns an idea that has been mashed from several others, and then reconstituted as its own thought? Even ten years ago, such actions might have elicited accusations of plagiarism, but today it is an assertion that ideas — and even their unique expression — cannot be owned.

It's no secret that appropriated ideas are second nature to a generation that grew up surfing information online, *a circuit with no defined beginning or end*. What is less understood is how that sort of cultivated distraction implicitly challenges goal-directedness. This shift has less to do with a wish to upend "morally sound attention" than an impulse for more immediate satisfaction. For those coming of age now, the linear effort of goal-directed thought is much less pleasurable than the buoyancy of floating from one focal point to the next. In this sort of mental orbit moments may be informed by images, sounds, or text, but all are impermanent by design. As a whole, they comprise a loop of continuously updated data points. The reason it's so hard to break away from surfing the net is that being in this real-time loop feels like participating, even when you're only spectating. The objective of the loop is not necessarily to *master* what one reads, so much as it is to *keep up*. The effect of this development poses a unique challenge: how do we motivate a generation whose momentum is more circuitous than linear? Does motivation have relevance for people who have abandoned traditional perspectives of progress?

Young people are increasingly sophisticated about using passivity to shield themselves from unwanted enthusiasms. Teenagers have a sixth sense for coercion, no matter how well it is disguised. They know when emotion is being used to ensnare them in a reality that is not of their own making. The evolutionary roots of this ability may be linked to physical survival: the essence of knowing whom to trust in life or death situations. Now, however, these perceptions are more fundamental to psychological survival, and especially the ability to maintain a *sovereign mind* in the presence of persistent attempts to persuade, or command.

The psychology of motivation is at the center of the disconnect between boomers and the next generation. My clinical work requires me to wrestle with this problem, although my belief in the benefits of *feeling motivated* is unequivocal. Motivated people are almost always a little happier than others; they typically convey an attachment to some sort of goal or belief that gives their life purpose and direction. Those benefits aside, the turbulence of becoming motivated is considerable. To go from being unmotivated to motivated is like turning oneself inside out. It demands flexibility, critical analysis of oneself, and a tolerance for discomfort. Most seriously, it usually requires the adoption of values — a hierarchy of purpose — that is, at least initially, not one's own.

It's not that the unmotivated don't or wouldn't enjoy feeling otherwise. The crux of the dilemma is that most people naturally resist hostile takeover. No matter how skillful the motivator, a small part of every healthy soul is opposed to submission. Adolescence is like putting that opposition on steroids. The resistance may surface as debate, procrastination, or outright refusal. Yet the underlying sentiment is much the same: nothing alien to "me" should inhabit "my" passions and effort. A basic instinct for self-preservation prevents a person from wanting to be *occupied* in that way. The overtures of adults fail because we don't see how motivation is an emotional transaction; *effortful behavior is exchanged for an outcome teenagers expect will make them feel more like their true selves.* People may become compliant when they get worn down, but they only agree to be motivated when the change taking place makes them feel like they have found a more natural state of being.

The best teachers and therapists consistently tap into this desire for personal truth as a means of cultivating connection. When young people hone in on their own truth, they experience a sense of congruity — the feeling that one's actions are consistent with one's core self. Congruity makes us feel more attuned to those things we value most. This could be our most prized personality traits, recreational interests, social or political values. We want others to recognize these differences — and honor them in relationships, communication, and teaching.

It feels good when someone tries to nurture congruity. That's why athletes submit to half-time pep talks, and why executives are stirred by the words of an executive coach. The person being motivated has faith that the advice will yield a *personally* desirable (congruent) outcome. And so apprehension is disarmed, and a person's needs for protection and open-mindedness can amiably commingle. This is good because we can no more live happily without occasionally being motivated than we can without sometimes feeling curious or confident. Ultimately, feeling motivated is a way of belonging to the world. The feeling of acceleration which motivation incurs is desirable, advantageous, and fun. Try to imagine being motivated without also feeling optimistic or capable.

~

The spirited have always been eager to "cure" the less endowed, even though their attempts at healing share a common, unarticulated premise: "be more like me and less like you." It's a problematic expectation, because it does not create an equitable or sustainable emotional transaction. It marginalizes appreciation of what a person wants for her or himself; is inherently unempathic, and easily detected by even the most inattentive adolescent. Adult angst *about* adolescence is at least as great as the angst of adolescence itself. The former borders on being a national obsession. It seems to reflect our discomfort with the chaos of freewheeling desire. In some cases, this is because our own desires are unresolved. Many adults plainly struggle with the high priority most adolescents place on gratification. For example, exactly how do "goals" intersect with adolescent priorities like having fun, being sexual, and wanting ample time for relaxation? Adolescence, while fertile ground for rapture, has a more contentious relationship with responsibility. It's a conflict that has to run its course, although there's no real consensus on where the course ends, and whether adults can have any meaningful effect.

As the pace of daily life accelerates, the image we hold for the able-bodied teen looks much more like mania than it does relaxed poise. We tend to be infatuated by people who exude energy and project a "can do" attitude. It may not occur to us to consider how our infatuation with energy expresses unspoken fears. For one, there is the fear of being left behind socially and economically. We may compensate with surface enthusiasm and frantic attention to detail. And there is also the fear of lacking any larger life purpose — in which case, *perpetual energy is an attractive substitute for meaning.* Energized people personify notions of success, and where energy can be translated into prosperity, the need for purpose is likely to go unattended. This is one reason why many anticipate a reflective search for self and meaning in retirement — once all the big money has been made, and upward mobility has lost a sense of urgency.

We tend to feel good about teens who are busy and "invested" in something. Our approval may outweigh concern as to whether the things a person does are congruent with a purposeful life. Overall, *what a person pursues, within reasonable limits, has become a less significant marker of wellbeing than the presence of pursuit itself.* Yet the anticipation of momentum in adolescence contrasts sharply with the ideals most adults seem to hold about early childhood. There is surely no critique of early childhood more ubiquitous than the notion that children are busy beyond reason.

Railing against such busyness is a way of expressing identification with wholesome values, even as we're burdened by guilt about the manic ambitions we may secretly hold for the young. Still, even if our guilt compels us to "let children be children," we're certainly not about to extend the same latitude to *adolescents*. Those who feel obligated to defend the absolute freedom of childhood are unlikely to have their own languishing, ear-budded teenagers in mind when they do so.

As a general rule, the value of a carefree childhood is beyond reproach until it is no longer advantageous to continued prosperity. Daycare is a practical example of this principle; as much as we might like for children to be with parents until they start school, that ideal doesn't always segue well with class aspirations among the upwardly mobile, or the immediate need for income faced by many others. With the onset of adolescence, it's even harder to stay the course. A bad report card lying ominously on the kitchen table has a way of suffocating relaxation and playfulness. Report cards and IQ scores have insidiously become symbols of a person's worth, and by pre-adolescence it's nearly impossible to get out from underneath this cloud.

Although young people are unlikely to fully understand the worry of those who raise them, it's not as though they don't feel the effects of those concerns. The stress implicit in being a 21st century teenager is enormous, and frequently has a paradoxical effect on teen behavior. Instead of boosting productive activity, stress contributes to withdrawal and, in some cases, stagnation. The result is a kind of inertia that is the untreatable aspect of what is routinely called ADHD.

There are no medical cures for a young person who finds school or entry-level jobs intolerably dull. For those whose lives are flattened by inertia, the subtext of distraction is an unwillingness to sit attentively in classrooms and jump through hoops of accomplishment that have been defined by someone else. If you're thinking these terms apply only to the few, I humbly ask you to consult your nearest high school. In my own research, young people robustly express their belief that the way to discover one's interests and talents is by trying new things. Yet this is the instinct conspicuously absent among the inert. The circularity of the situation is maddening. The very actions that could lift tentative young people from the constricting effects of doubt and apprehension are beyond reach *because* of doubt and apprehension.

Inertia amplifies the natural ambivalence of youth, making it that much more difficult to know what's worth doing. And an absence of self-knowledge, or authenticity, is a major source of personal anxiety. Some believe that social networks like Facebook negate the relevance of authenticity. There may be those who view authenticity as an outdated notion of self-discovery that clashes with the malleability of identities enabled by social media. It's clear that young people can, and do, reinvent themselves with the push of a button. But exercise of that impulse does not establish that authenticity is irrelevant. It seems more accurate to say that the value of deeply knowing oneself has been obstructed by the speed and flux with which young people interact. When those impediments are removed, such as in small group dialogues or psychotherapy, young people can become riveted by an opportunity to excavate those more enduring aspects of their personalities, and the values that define them.

Even so, most teens need to embark on this sort of discovery with someone who has no stake in what gets revealed. Parents may be the people most invested in the outcome of the exploration, but that relationship is so full of projections it's usually hard to know who is setting the agenda, or why. Humanist and psychologist Carl Rogers emphasized that authenticity is built on the observation of facts (personal experience) without judgment. This is never more true than during adolescence.

Many young people turn to their friends in times of doubt, and a few find themselves in a therapist's office. But in the latter case the person facing them may appear alien, owing to generational differences. Therapy authenticity assumes its real relevance when the junior member of the conversation becomes insistent on digging it out. Usually, this is an open-ended dialogue to which a person returns over the course of years. Those years don't necessarily have to be spent in psychotherapy, but most young people need a baseline of continuity that allows personal exploration to remain on track — to lead somewhere. For many, we need to interrupt the continuous "loop," and return to a more traditional concept of knowledge; one that evolves over time. The events of youth comprise the unique history of one person's coming of age. It is frankly tragic when those experiences are unexplored; as if becoming a person could occur without witness and communication.

Every adolescent needs someone to serve that critical need. This imperative also underscores the essential contribution of memory to maturity, and is beautifully conveyed through Navajo wisdom: "Remember what you have seen, because everything forgotten returns to the circling winds." Those "circling winds" are perilously similar to the circuits of online culture, which inherently foster forgetfulness. And forgetfulness is an enemy of authenticity. We become more authentic, in part, by putting memories in order; by creating narratives that propel us forward with greater certainty about what we seek.

Practically speaking, a young adult's search for authenticity should include reckoning with responsibility for one's basic needs. Authenticity is not a seminar at a prestigious school; it is a quest to know the fundamental chunks of one's personhood — what can't be discarded without violating the integrity of who one is. Today, however, few seriously entertain the notion that they will perish from neglect of such needs. The irony of this situation is that the safety net so many take for granted makes early adulthood feel pathologically precious. It delays the need for decision-making. It stunts maturity. Consider, for example, the difficulty a college student might have in declaring a major, or a twenty-something in choosing a career. Now compare that sort of vacillation with the decisiveness evinced by young people a century ago. We might argue that the prospects for true happiness were more remote then, and therefore didn't warrant much contemplation. But even just a few generations ago, happiness wouldn't have been thought of as an experience to be cultivated for its own sake. Instead, it was the effect of a life well lived, and clearly subordinate to the pragmatic requirements of survival. Because the attainment of basic needs is mostly taken for granted in first world nations, many young people have become lost in a surfeit of possibilities about how to allocate their time. It's a maze that edges the mind toward solipsism rather than pleasure. No one wishes for a life of hardship, yet that constriction has historically made the lunge for escape feel exciting. Accordingly, political oppression spurs evocative art, and economic desperation inspires impassioned new music.

By contrast, a person freed from all risk and responsibility is cast adrift, with no particular urgency to row this way or that. It is another permutation of endless circling with no obvious destination. Consider as well those whose lives have not benefitted from great protection, such as being affected by serious illness, poverty, or combat trauma, and how they convey a greater degree of maturity, albeit painfully won.

Psychological Freedom

Popular conceptions of freedom generally refer to political dimensions of life, such as the degree to which a person's actions are independent of state interference or consequences. Milton Friedman, as economist and social philosopher, suggested that economic freedom must exist first, for political freedom to be enacted, and become meaningful.[1] History, however, suggests that the transactional structure of most societies makes economic freedom contingent upon some forms of compromise. The essential compromises consist of acknowledging social hierarchies, and engaging the "rules" those systems assert as a condition for employment. For the most part, changes in political power, such as elections, have less immediate relevance to individual liberties than the effects of the average workplace. Primarily these are liberties having to do with attitude and disposition. Being a competent worker is rarely enough for an employer; most employees are also expected to carry out their job with the proper disposition. The suppression implicit in this hired attitude is a compromise one makes to be gainfully employed. It's an expectation levied of virtually anyone who works; equally true of a retail manager, an offshore teletech, and an actor working a day job.

Even where organizations invite free thinking, there is an implicit expectation that those free thoughts will be focused on the wellbeing of the organization. This is the dilemma that stirs late adolescence, and which is foreshadowed by the experience of going to school. The young may be surrounded by energy and positive emotion, but the problem is that much of that enthusiasm is not of their own making. The inertia that young people experience in response to this situation has layers. One of its most central meanings is *a refusal to resolve the conflict between the need for economic stability and the need for autonomy*. By opting out of traditional forms of ambition, the young try to circumvent the stress of this conflict. Many have hunkered down, unwilling to adopt the attitude and emotional suppression that define popular conceptions of maturity. The consolation prize, and prospective consequence of this refusal, are much the same: a delay of responsibility, and the extension of adolescence.

Opting out of work-for-pay lifestyles prolongs the freedom of adolescence, and it also deflates the bubble of prosperity. The economy, as constructed, depends on the young to be productive and to consume. The urgency of these expectations causes adults to feel anxious and impatient. Accordingly, our response to hesitant adolescents is more mechanistic than empathic. It is generally more insistent than inquiring. These differences in attitude are deeply encoded within our speech, facial expressions, and body language. And they are unmistakable "tells" to those hanging out on the other side of the generational divide.

In most nations, and certainly in the United States, medical culture plays a dominant role in shaping taxonomies of unwanted, undesirable behavior. The distress that these behaviors cause individuals and societies is the basis for finding them to be pathological. Doctors rely on the clarity of that distinction as grounds for providing treatment. It is, overall, an efficient system that results in the management or elimination of various mental ailments. But one rather slippery effect of pathologizing an individual's behavior is that the "problem" is conceptualized as existing *within the mind of the afflicted*. Even where the problem has been caused by social-psychological circumstances, the problem is treated as though it is physically contained within an individual mind. Thinking of inertia as a dysfunction of the cortex may structure our understanding of the problem's genesis, but offers little in the way of a remedy.

Remarkably, feelings of resistance and skepticism may be *ego-syntonic*. This means those feelings may not be unwanted, and might even feel good. Of course it can be argued that being stuck or hesitant is not in a person's long-term interest, but that's not the main concern of the afflicted. Like an anorectic who refuses to eat, an adolescent who has purposely slowed her or his own passage into adulthood has discovered personal power through passive resistance. It's a distorted but powerful association that can be difficult to revise. Those who are stuck long enough may eventually inhabit that outlook, becoming so comfortable with inertia that it feels like home.

Searching for Congruity

So, do young people affected by refusal, or at least hesitation, have irreconcilable differences with the world beyond themselves? More specifically, are we to conclude that the trajectory of youth is perpendicular to the needs of a robust economy? It might be tempting to reach this conclusion, but that would be predicated on a skewed map of adolescence — one that does not show their desire for passionate belief in something. Retreat from a hierarchical path to prosperity may be a genuine reflex, but it's also prompted by flighty assumptions. For example, the belief that the good life is a matter of luck. This is not a shy or self-effacing definition of the good life, and it's not decadence and entitlement either. It is honest confusion steeped in revolt.

The best hope for such a life is to make congruence the centerpiece of one's important choices. This sort of approach doesn't necessarily require the realization of personal fantasies, but it does require that building a life around what one enjoys, and identifies with, is a viable possibility. Belief in that possibility is the basis of allowing oneself to be motivated; the absence of this belief is the essence of the *motivation gap* the distance between opting out and a commitment to full immersion.

A failing economy makes the possibility of congruity seem even more remote, and it's a problem more complex than simply needing any job. Annually, a small army of new college graduates marches forward with the hope that their work-life will, in some meaningful way, reflect their educational choices. In many cases, these choices are far more personal than opportunistic. They represent the soul of a person's hope for him or herself, a way to transcend the drudgery of merely working to live. For decades we have accepted that English majors are not entitled to jobs as writers. Are we now ready to assume the corollary of those studying law, computer science, education, and civil engineering?

Opportunity to pursue happiness through vocation is essential because more routine forms of contentment — especially those derived from self-reliance — have been in steep decline for decades. Few of us have lives that include any sense of hands-on urgency or necessity. Self-reliance has evolved to mean the earning of enough money to sustain whatever lifestyle a person has decided is satisfactory. Yet that achievement is still a considerable leap from congruity. Pursuit of a better coordinated, fulfilling life expresses belief in the capacity of work to be transcendent. We work not only to live, but to fulfill our potential for creative industry. In such work we find reason and reward — a way out of inertia, toward a more sustainable happiness. This is an equation at odds with modern ideas about success and the path to prosperity. The narrative of upward mobility leverages the wants of the individual as motivation to comply with what is best for the economy and its primary beneficiaries. Whether this leverage occurs in actual workplaces, or is simply the effect of social mores that govern a person's work ethic and consumption, the basic intent is to reinforce compliance.

Opposing this approach is a half-century of social science research concluding that a fire ignited from within burns longer than one sparked by external rewards. Despite the evidence, the most common approaches to motivating the young are organized around contingency systems emphasizing rewards for good behavior. The liability here lies in positioning "good" as a set of actions absent any degree of authorship. What message do we send adolescents and young adults when we reinforce behavior that is void of any investment of self? Isn't the resulting message that compliance trumps expression? Can this approach conceivably yield happiness or true motivation? Just as middle age workers hunger for more meaningful acknowledgment than the approval of having successfully followed work protocols, young people need to have their selves recognized apart from the civil, compliant behavior they demonstrate at home and school.

When a teenager's compliance and self-worth are conflated — by even well-meaning adults — intrinsic motivation is suffocated. This is the essential problem of receiving a report card in school. As adults, we may view grades as a marker of socioeconomic potential, but that abstraction has little immediate relevance for students. The co-evolution of adolescence and economic productivity highlights the interdependence of lifestyle and prosperity. The current shortage of entry-level jobs is accelerating that change, but the real catalyst for this transformation is the demand of young minds that work be made more playful and personally relevant. The hub of youth now working their way into the economy are doing reconnaissance for this effort. The most dramatic changes will occur because adolescents do not feel tethered to the vision of prosperity created by their parents and grandparents. The new ecology of adolescence and early adulthood calls into question the very values upon which ideas of success have traditionally been based. Paradoxically, our best hope for a prosperous future may be pinned to the young being successful in making the inclinations of their psyches economically, and therefore socially, viable.

Habits of mind, including the structure and tempo of thought, are less likely to be constrained by moral imperatives handed down from previous generations. Whatever trail to prosperity the next generation blazes will have to accommodate these new habits of mind, because they have grown too strong to be suppressed by human will. Many young people have already come to grips with this transformation, and are now searching for ways to live more faithfully to these generational changes. It's possible that taking medication to improve attention will soon become a form of nostalgia. The next generation seems more likely to engage ways of getting into distraction, than trying to figure out how to control it.

The current intersection of mind and economy invites both caution and wonder. Young people interest us as a generation, as much as they worry us as our progeny. It's difficult to imagine we will give up our desire to nurture them in our own image. Yet that hasn't stopped the next generation from sensing that there are new rules governing happiness, and work. Embedded in the changing face of prosperity is a softer fusion of life and work; an ideal that identity, values, and behavior do not have to be falsely compartmentalized. It's more than a trivial wish; it's a belief in the possibility of belonging to the world, without compromise. Inside that hope, worry about the economy, and where one will fit in, are manageable.

The Case for Boredom

O URS IS AN UNCIVIL AGE. Entertainers rationalize incivility as part of the show; your offense only
indicates a defective, un-hip sense of humor. Politicians
reframe incivility as moral indignation in the service of
the public good. Public incivility now defines the national
character as much as independence, perseverance, and
prosperity.

The decline of civility encompasses the erosion of
manners, but extends beyond manners alone. Manners
are more or less matters of habit — reflexes that require
little premeditation. In contrast, civility requires not only
courteous action, but empathic intention. It is the distilled
spirit of concern for the emotions of others that guides
common rules of civil social engagement. In Cormac
McCarthy's *No Country for Old Men*, an aging sheriff reflects on the savage violence taking place in his west Texas
town, explaining, "It starts when you begin to overlook
bad manners. Anytime you quit hearin' 'sir' and 'ma'am,'
the end is pretty much in sight."

Instilling civility is at the center of my vocation as a
psychologist. For more than a decade I have wrestled with
helping school-age children to understand how to lead
civil lives. This work can be both intensely frustrating and

extremely rewarding. It has brought me face to face with the evolving nature of childhood, and has made plain the ways that the little niceties of life that we usually take for granted — polite greetings, sincere apologies, expressions of gratitude and sympathy — are essential to civilized life.

For some years, I worked with small groups of boys, seven or eight at a time, in a kind of therapy typically referred to as a "social-skills group." Through discussion with families and schools, I found I could identify and gather a group of boys with tendencies toward impulsivity, rudeness, and social indifference; I could then present an alternative set of strategies for coping with self-defeating thoughts, urges, and behavior; and finally, I could coach the boys to apply those skills in their daily lives. My work now mostly involves studying young people's social and cognitive development, and contributing to the international and cross-cultural dialogue about contemporary youth. With some perspective on my former work, I still believe that my initial approach was worthwhile, although I can now better appreciate the ways that young minds are equipped to resist this type of learning.

Confronted with the difficulty of conveying the relevance of civil behavior to boys and young men, it's easy to feel discouraged by their moral ambivalence. One wonders why these boys don't care about how they are perceived, or what makes them feel as though empathy is optional. And although such questions are relevant concerns for the psychology of boys in general, civility has a more formidable nemesis — one that is on the attack and growing stronger by the day.

Among most schoolchildren, incivility and the demise

of social skills have much less to do with rebellion and the preferred diagnosis of "oppositionality" than they do with the annihilation of boredom. Fifty years ago, the onset of boredom might have followed a two-hour stretch of nothing to do. In contrast, boys today can feel bored after thirty seconds with nothing specific to do; the threshold has been drastically lowered. Their lives are now filled with electronica — games, phones, computers — an updated version of the old counterculture mantra "turn on, tune in, drop out." The beeps, buzzes, and cryptic messages of electronic feedback are ever-present, and many boys want nothing to do with moderation. This ubiquitous, battery-powered cacophony of multisensory junk food can hold boys spellbound for hours.

The choices of adolescents, in particular, are prone to inverse intuition. The adolescent mind is now so hyper-stimulated that the absence of stimulation — boredom — is unsettling, while the chaos of constant connection is soothingly familiar. A languishing teenager feels irritable and instinctively knows how to rev up: go online, turn on the TV, call someone, text. Continuous stimulation and communication comprise the new normal. It is a state of being that conflates sensory pleasure with happiness. Meanwhile, the gaps *between* moments of heightened stimulation have been shrunk, and are on the verge of disappearing altogether. Consequently, virtually all waking cognition is now of the highest intensity for a great majority of young people. Electronica has squeezed the boredom out of life. It makes us crave more of what makes us sick, like an addiction.

As the synaptic mindscape of daily life becomes increasingly marked by peaks and the disappearance of valleys, we might reasonably expect to see some signs of distress among the hyper-stimulated. But that doesn't seem to be the case. Instead, we are witnessing an adaptation so massive and rapid that it raises the question of where disorder really lies: when the Centers for Disease Control and Prevention estimate that many millions of Americans meet the diagnostic criteria for Attention-Deficit/Hyperactivity Disorder, this putative disorder is arguably no longer a disorder at all — it's just the way we are.

No one likes to be bored — indeed, boredom so deeply invades the mind-body system that bored children sometimes feel queasy or lethargic; they may complain of headaches. But the occurrence of boredom in young minds would be a welcome sign in one respect — it would suggest the presence of available resources for thought, reflection, and civil behavior. By extension, there is a relationship between the elimination of opportunities for boredom and the rise of incivility. While boredom is hardly something to strive for, its presence confirms the existence of brief gaps in the continuous stimulation that dominates the thinking cycle of many kids. These pauses enable thought and reason to infuse action; *they* are boredom's natural habitat, and the genesis of civil behavior. It is only during moments of relative calm that young minds learn to bind empathy to action, and the development of thoughtful behaviors we associate with civility.

Although the civility drain is widely apparent among youth, it isn't only because of electronica. Among a great many boys, civility and social skills are often greeted as a slog of irrelevant, artificial etiquette. This is in part because the preponderance of boys between the ages of eleven and fourteen associate civility with subordination. Civility feels like submission or servitude to these boys and as such is inconsistent with their idealized selves. Boys' minds inhabit a world of evocative images and narratives that influence their behavior. These images and stories, the personal mythologies of boyhood, have more to do with a longing for autonomy, power, and superiority than an appreciation of civic interdependence. To an extent, boys are affected by the public examples of incivility that they routinely encounter at school, on television, and elsewhere. These role models release a child from the burden of his own conscience, and drown out whatever kindness he may have come by naturally. Remarkably, we still want children to be kind toward each other, as though such intentions should magically spring from the essential goodness of childhood.

In contrast, civility is constructed brick by brick, one example at a time. Being civil is rarely fun — it requires patience, forethought, and some willingness to tolerate tedium. While happiness and contentment are civility's ally, fun, as defined by the relentless quest for pleasure, is tragically its foe. For all the billions of hours devoted to electronic fun, does anyone think that young people have become happier?

I sometimes worry that therapy is no match for the effects of electronica on young male cognition. In this new topography of mind, boredom isn't just dull; it is out of sync with the tempo many boys have come to associate with strength and wellness. Like a car whose idle is set too low, bored boys feel as though they are about to stall. They may try to triage with sugary, caffeinated drinks, but will have a hard time satisfying themselves until they have a device in hand. And as boys become men, those who find boredom entirely intolerable will sublimate by testing the limits of physical endurance, or perhaps even seeking a rush by experimenting with drugs or otherwise breaking the law. By then, the prospect of civility will have long since passed. It is when boys are still boys that we have a practical chance of shaping their conception of manliness, and of making civility a part of that vision.

Teaching civility often feels like swimming against the tide, and in my sessions I'm always vulnerable to feeling awkward or embarrassed by boys' reactions. Sometimes it's like I'm back in middle school myself, and I feel priggish for suggesting a topic the boys view as alien or emasculating. But that vulnerability has helped me to appreciate the awkwardness that punctuates the social lives of boys. That is the place where civility begins in our groups: not just as an idea, but as a living example learned one interaction at a time.

Civility requires intelligence less than it does patience and a willingness to put the brakes on when you feel like accelerating. For those who might wonder, change *is* possible. I have watched difficult boys become promising young men, and witnessed how the perception of civility is transformed from something alien to a chance for honor.

Few of us enjoy boredom, yet the availability of mental

space that boredom represents goes hand in hand with a civil mind. We should cling to the pauses in cognition that boredom signals as we might cling to a life raft. It may be our last hope for a private moment of time and space — a chance to breathe and consider how to treat others, before the prospect of civility drowns in a wave of electronic thrills, and there's no air left to think.

On Monstrous Children

MODERN CHILDREN face an unfortunate fact. For all the love and attention lavished on them, hardly a soul takes them seriously. Further, despite abundant indulgence and protection provided to middle-class children in particular, few are given anything significant to do, because few adults believe there is very much they *can* do. Accordingly, their serious thoughts on matters of daily consequence are rarely invited. I suspect that the suggestion that this is a problem may strike some as absurd. Yet the loud repercussions of this state of affairs are considerable, and we should address how this imbalance now colors the temperament of childhood. Usually, our society focuses intensely on the effect, while paying less attention to the cause of children's behavior. So there is ample discussion of the most pressing problems: poor attitude, impulsive self-gratification, aggression, and elements of depression. It is not my intention to suggest that such syndromes don't exist, because they do, hindering the harmony to which most families and classrooms aspire.

When such problems occur, however, it is unproductive and nonsensical to address them out of context, and irrespective of whether or not a child has ever been *held* in serious regard. This is a kindred "holding environment" to the one identified by D.W. Winnicott, and amplified by others among the British object-relations school of psychoanalysts in the early 20th century. Where providing a safe and stable emotional environment was a sufficient foundation for good parenting seventy-five years ago, today's children seem to call out for something more interactive. Whether this call reflects the evolving complexity of childhood, or an escalation in children's egocentrism is debatable. But however this need has emerged, it now poses a challenge to established ways of thinking about parenting and teaching, and the psychological needs of children.

Spiraling behavior problems infect not only adult-child relations in the form of frank rudeness, tantrums, and oppositionality; they also include stunning and increasingly prevalent acts of cruelty toward other children. Bullying, for example, has infiltrated cliques once believed to be relatively impervious to antisocial group-think. At some point in the past thirty days, most of us will have likely heard about a group of ostensibly normal children who banned together for the sole purpose of tormenting another child, maybe to the point of death.

In an age of behaviorism, the prevailing belief is that psychological problems are best resolved by changing how people act, and by attempting to tweak with medicine whatever neuro-anomalies trigger those actions. It's a well intended approach, that reflects our preference for algorithmic efficiency in discussing social problems. But the myopia of behaviorism can, in some cases, have the undesirable effect of oversimplifying human psychology.

Some think of children as only slightly more sophisticated than their pets. It is not a coincidence that the books of Cesar Millan, a bestselling author on dog behavior, are now also consulted with respect to raising children.[1] These are readable texts, free of the complexity inherent in relating to a being whose selfhood is shaped by semantics, and how words may confer or deny power and status.

In comparison with the techniques of a dog behaviorist, a psychology of more density, and pertaining to something as mysterious as childhood, might be considerably less attractive. Children's emotional issues are time consuming, and involve a degree of moral ambiguity about what or who has caused the problem. They require one to think about language. Is the meaning of what I say the same as what is heard? And for the very youngest — who have limited vocabularies but big appetites for *understanding* — how exactly is the meaning of communication derived?

The youngest members of our society have a deeply felt need to be taken seriously. The monstrous behavior of some children is a response to the absence of such seriousness. In this regard, behavior problems are better understood along a social axis, than as a matter of personal discontentment existing within an individual child. The most important premise of this perspective is that behavior is immediately and powerfully influenced by how one is regarded by other people. Specifically, to be taken seriously is to be acknowledged and respected for your *differences, priorities,* and *abilities*; it is to be held in focused consideration, and given reasonable opportunity to influence the momentum of your life. Although such a possibility may be a psycho-spiritual ideal, it has some notable political parallels.

For instance, when Thomas Jefferson declares the "pursuit of happiness" to be an unalienable right of Americans, albeit certain *adult* Americans, he seems to be tapping the yearning for felicity felt by citizens of an emerging republic. And yet viewed through the lens of the present, Jefferson's prescription appeals as much to the psychological need for self-determination as it does to the notion of a democratic republic. Here, in the 21st century, we can also see how the right to self-determination is as essential to the young as it is to adults.

The social status of society's youngest members has changed, primarily because they are now less willing to experience their needs as subordinate, or as a transitional phase to a more authoritative time of life. For one, children are asked to remain passive and directed for decades before they get to apply their instinct for autonomy. There's little consideration of the possibility that a child feels called to do or learn a particular thing. It's a situation that has led to a new type of childhood malaise, with larger numbers of children feeling chronically disappointed or irritated. These emotions have most certainly always been a part of childhood, but the extent to which they now shape children's consciousness is striking. For example, in my clinical work I now find myself talking to children quite matter-of-factly about what "annoys" them. It's a conversational focal point that emerges in response to their impatience and irritability — a matter about which they are often well aware and indignant. The fluency which children bring to such dialogue makes it clear that they have consolidated a clear understanding of how their subjective desires are out of sorts with what actually happens in their lives. Some children are annoyed with not *always* getting what they want. True, such conflicts may not be particularly new, but the advancement of children's self-awareness has led them to feel entitled enough to stand their ground when conflicts do occur.

This confident assertiveness is particularly evident among middle-class children. They have typically had abundant exposure to self-interested verbal sparring, and have acquired the belief that making some semblance of a reasoned argument is the same as actually having a particular right. This is a class and generation that knows how to conduct business with language, and which does not associate assertive self-advocacy with shame. There may be no viable way to reverse this trend, and there are reasons we may not wish to turn back even if we could. But we can learn to respond to children more constructively, in a way that addresses the crux of the problem. We can, for example, neutralize a lot of nuisance behavior by zeroing in on the thing that children want most — to be taken seriously.

Incredible Childhoods

Almost no one, including the best doctors and therapists, likes to be around children with monstrous behavior. Whether one is a parent or professional, these children have an uncanny ability to make you feel incompetent in a hurry. How should we speak to this miniature terrorist, destroying personal property, and sporting a Scooby-Doo band-aid? Anxiety and rash reaction may quickly follow. The most dire of these reactions is to medicate every symptom that can't be handled with a "time-out." That's a search and destroy approach, and it misses the true cause of monstrous behavior. Seriousness is unfortunately a concept out-of-sync with modern notions about what causes a child to be "good," or what helps him or her to feel happy. And seriousness cannot be resolved on the fly, in between other activities, or with the help of a digital device. There is no app to fix monstrous behavior. Its cause is a disconnect between the social atmosphere of childhood, and the way children actually want to feel about themselves. Although many savvy parents sense this disconnect, most have been left feeling alone in their frustration because there is no broader discussion of how the meaning of childhood is changing.

One significant hurdle is that current ideas about childhood have been tainted by a zeitgeist of indulgence. This is a way of compensating children for being one among many, to confer specialness in an overcrowded world. Yet indulgence contributes to a mental vacuum in which things and personal attention are conflated with wellbeing. Because safety is now harder to attain, it is increasingly understood as a reward for being middle-class. The effect of this emphasis is that safety now squarely trumps the value of experience and experimentation. Would anyone argue with the assertion that our basic associations with "risk" are negative? Try free associating with "risk," and see if anything comes to mind faster than "reduce," or "high." And so we have reduced risk, making life somewhat more shallow at the same time. That doesn't necessarily stop us, however, from romanticizing about a time when risk was a more natural occurrence in life, or from occasionally reflecting on how to package sensible risk for the young. Families with expendable income, for example, will find numerous wilderness camps eager to tame wild children by enforcing physical activity, chores, and self-reliance. My own work with families suggests that some of these programs work quite well, although it leaves one to wonder if those less fortunate may simply have to endure the public humiliation of badly behaved children, or rely on pharmaceuticals to help "raise" them.

Monstrous behavior has multiple permutations, even if its understanding is at present quite narrow. Consider that it is obviously monstrous to commit acts of aggression leading to physical and emotional pain in others, but it can also be monstrous to initiate an embarrassing tantrum in a public place, and then resist all forms of earnest consolation. The common denominator of such acts is being consumed by urgent, unchecked, emotional upset. At such moments, a child is turned inside out, unhappiness circulating through every cell of the body, his or her behavior never more childish or unreasonable. When this behavior is rare, parents are inclined to appease, but where the outpouring of grief is more chronic — and inexplicable — their own anger might overcome available reserves of empathy. This is particularly so when there is no diagnosis to provide a reason why the child behaves this way, other than that he or she is "strong willed."

Responding to monstrous behavior is an emotional transaction, and a bit like a game of "chicken." You can never be sure who'll flinch first. Preventing that behavior, however, has more to do with applying empathy before emotions spiral out of control. Practically speaking, we convey earnest empathy by signaling — with voice, face, and body — an attitude of serious consideration. Please note the distinction here: we can convey empathy without acting sympathetic. This is because seriousness, rather than merely the acknowledgment of feelings, is what the child desires. These elements of communication facilitate relationship, and convey the credibility children covertly or overtly crave. And in fact, many childhoods are now quite literally *incredible*, which is to say they lack an atmosphere of seriousness and authenticity.

Consider how few children are offered an opportunity to do important things; this is an existential void that translates into scarce opportunity to be needed, to fulfill a meaningful role within the context of family, school, and community. I appreciate that it may seem a stretch to think about childhood as a matter of such weighty philosophical concerns, but there is no other viable path to restoring childhood's equilibrium. Without a tether to *purpose* and *need*, childhood lacks essential gravity. More plainly, life can become absurdly arbitrary; things are done less for a purpose than because they are fun, distracting, or because one is bored. We cannot insulate children by giving them ever more stuff. Does this sound familiar? In such societies, childhood is hollowed of its meaning and potential for joy. I believe children are in revolt about this situation, although I recognize this is an uncoordinated effort, fought one meltdown at a time.

Respect-ABILITY

Years of talking closely with children suggests that they have an innate awareness of what one needs to grow. They can also sense that current priorities are askew, and signs of rebellion are everywhere. Consider that angry, explosive youth have inspired thousands of pages of professional advice. A recent study by researchers from Harvard Medical School examined the lives of over six thousand adolescents, and found that two-thirds had a history of extreme anger and threatening violence.[2] And among primary school students, it is often the most unruly children who command the lion's share of attention and resources. Agitated children can make one so uneasy as to inspire fantasies about banishing them, making them go away until they have realized how hurtful and humiliating their monstrous behavior has been. It is reported by the Yale Child Study Center that preschool children are more likely to be expelled from school than any other age group.[3] Although such behavior among the very young is not necessarily new, it does seem more common today. Our collective response to the situation is widely known, and begs the question as to whether a preponderance of schools could function any longer without the sedating or focusing effects of pharmaceuticals. I am not unsympathetic to families or schools who view such intervention as essential to carrying on with their principle business. But are we not descending the slipperiest of slopes, and does the pace of our descent preclude sufficient consideration of both individuals and medical consequences?

As a psychologist, I'm often asked to explain the origins of this impertinence, and fix disrespectful children. These are tense conversations that converge upon certain truths. For example, that respect can only thrive when it is mutual. One can't take respect, and it is rarely offered without clear indication it will be reciprocated. To be disrespected — to have your esteem set on fire — ignites red feelings, the sort of anger that makes someone feel belittled and infuriated all at once.

Disrespect always feels bad, but coming from someone younger — perhaps not old enough to tie her shoes, or who derives his worldview from cartoon animals — causes special irritation. It doesn't feel logical, because as adults we presume the right to be respected by children. Intensifying this expectation is the general scarcity of respect in all types of contemporary relationships. It's a siege that has most of us in a state of persistent deprivation, and thus ravenous for signs of deference, whether at home or work, with family or friends. Disrespect is a fundamental reason for rage in our world, and it should come as no surprise that the epidemic has spread to childhood.

We all want to know that others take us seriously, and when it comes to children we often demand this attitude. But children get angry for many of the same reasons we do, and there is a ricochet to these emotions that resists a quick fix. Succinctly, *the monstrously disrespectful behavior of children is essentially their response to feeling disrespected themselves*. Still, we might reasonably wonder, "shouldn't respect have to be earned?" The short answer is no. One should not have to "earn" a basic human need.

Withholding respect until it has been earned is as grave as refusing to hug a child until he or she has proven lovable. Children learn to give genuine respect through living example, and they can't return what hasn't been given to them first.

I know that many were brought up with a different ethos, the notion that respect *must* be earned, and that the giving and receiving of respect is governed by the hierarchies of age and status. Yet this perspective has lost its traction, and provides no practical help with current circumstances. Consider a key misunderstanding of what is implied by respect. Where children are concerned, it doesn't mean the right to make one's own rules, but it does suggest that children have a right (and need) to be considered as individuals, distinct from their age group. This is no different than adults wanting to be understood — to have our needs considered — apart from markers of age, gender or demography.

With respect to children, we are feeding their need for individuation and seriousness with indulgence — stuffing them full of things and experiences in compensation for a lack of time or interest in knowing them better. This is a direction in childrearing which encourages an enlarged sense of self, without grounding that selfhood in anything beyond the satisfaction of personal desires, or expression of personal styles. Objecting to the scale of expectations children hold for themselves may feel righteous, but it defies logic and prima facie evidence of childhood's evolution. For example, contemporary children are notably larger than recent generations, and cognitive research suggests they're measurably smarter as well.[4] I suspect few would view those changes as moral failings.

I'm not advocating for a cheapened version of respect, or suggesting that we should accept monstrous behavior. My argument has a more specific premise: *monstrous behavior has gravity beyond being a nuisance; it cannot be rectified without recalibrating our coordinates as a society, including an acknowledgment that childhood is now shaped by a complex demand for significance.*

There is presently great concern about the sudden shortage of empathy among children, an attribute broadly understood as the linchpin of social competence. It's a phenomenon that was initially associated with the epidemic of autism, but which now appears to be associated with the syndrome of "childhood" itself. It seems that every small town needs a psychologist offering training in social skills. (I have been such a person in my small town.) Although nurturing empathy may enhance social competence, its ultimate value is much greater. Empathy is the core of a civil society. The frequency of extremely bad behavior among children is a prominent sign of civility's decline, and it's hard to imagine how civility can be restored other than through a top-down demonstration project in which children are held in serious regard.

Describing what that should look like is inherently risky. Formulaic interpretations of seriousness or respect may have the unfortunate effect of limiting imagination and suggesting that one size fits all — the very antithesis of serious regard. With due caution, however, I would like to suggest some starting points:

1   Listen intently with an open mind, even when
    your every instinct prompts you to disagree
    emphatically.

2   Ask serious questions often, inviting a child's moral
    perspective on a variety of important issues, inside
    and outside of family concerns.

3   Require children to do difficult things which
    are congruent with their own interests and
    inclinations.

I have described this last element elsewhere as *purposeful work*, tasks that add up to more than school work and chores. The key is to assign work that elevates a person's sense of him or herself. In that ascendance, children find a reason to be more flexible, more willing to consider the needs of others.

A persistent lack of seriousness in a child's relationship with adults feels like insignificance. A half-century ago, these feelings might have been acceptably suppressed because the division between childhood and adulthood was unambiguous, and shorter in duration. But today, children are more savvy about their personal capabilities, and are able to demonstrate them in areas like technology, performance arts, and sports. It's more difficult to suppress one's esteem and independence with an awareness of substantial capability in hand. Even children whose accomplishments lag behind are aware of what's being done by their most exemplary peers, and they are emboldened by that awareness. A ten-year-old who watches a documentary on a ten-year-old genius quickly assimilates the idea that children her age are sometimes smarter than adults. That awareness affects her sensibilities, and may emerge in her debating efforts. The key hurdles for young people are how to give respect without sacrificing self-esteem, to understand that respect is social currency, and (for teenagers, especially) that cooperation is not optional in a functional society. These manifestations of empathy build civil societies.

Plotting New Coordinates

We may think of bad behavior among our youngest as a symptom of entitlement, but the hubris of the pack has more to do with frustration about not being taken seriously, than it does with having been spoiled. Children in most western societies are waiting to be asked to do something important; to apply themselves to a viable task that will yield a visible, meaningful result. This sort of industry will necessarily look somewhat different from one child to the next, but the underpinning of all such efforts is a universal hunger "to do," and to be recognized as worthy and capable. Inclusion in purposeful work signifies respect; it grounds a person in the here and now, and gives them a place of significance in the community of others. It is inherently social. In some cases, it takes longer to complete a task with a young helper, and in other cases, children have initial enthusiasm but haven't developed the habits of mind to fully participate. But such tabulations miss the larger point of inclusion, and do not account for how cooperative, goal-directed experiences give one's life meaning and focus. We expect school to provide all these opportunities, and while some are doing a fine job within shrinking parameters, communities and parents are where, figuratively and literally, most of the work needs to be done. Constructive action under the attentive and approving gaze of a parent is an irreplaceable experience. How else does a society implant a value for industry? What can we buy that could conceivably be more powerful, or more memorable?

The monstrous behavior of small children is not a failing on the part of individuals as much as it is the failing of a society to embrace the realism of childhood. I've learned that many boys have never used tools, and even fewer say that they have ever participated in making something beautiful.[5] My sense is that many children hesitate when presented an opportunity because they doubt the outcome will be good enough — worthy of the effort. Illusions of perfection victimize parents as much as children, and keep us chronically dissatisfied with real life. The pressing need for child therapy reflects the vicious effects of perfection myths; if we can't be perfect, we at least need somewhere to vent, and to be reassured that perfection is not normal.

Moving from a place of subjectivity to objectivity is a major task of growing up. But how can we foster that change in young people if we don't take them more seriously? Children want and demand this consideration, and in receiving it they find a sign that the power and authority of adults is not absolute. This is no small realization on their part. It is a sign that they can exist as a significant person, even while growing up within a system in which they lack full autonomy.

We may assume that children have no right to respect but *the permeability of adult power is received as an essential form of acceptance in a child's life*. Until this need is tangibly acknowledged, we leave children detached from a degree of regard that signifies meaningful inclusion. Monstrous behavior is the sound of discontent with this isolation. It will be difficult for any community of adults to effectively respond to this call without first reckoning with the state of respect in their own lives. And that's as it should be. The themes of childhood have always been a kind of cultural compass, a chance for adults to look inward at the same moment we seek remedies for the youngest.

This is a cultural moment of unique gravity, and one worthy of complex reflection. The shape of relations between parents and children, and teachers and children, is now drawn according to different parameters. It is unreasonable to expect that the will of childhood can be restrained by hierarchy, order, and medication, no matter how consistently they are applied. The outward compliance of children should not be mistaken for a surrender of will. Our wellbeing as societies, now and in the future, rests upon accepting new coordinates in which age does not disqualify one for respect or individual consideration. The rewards of this effort are a civil society; a place where respect is freely offered, and where one doesn't have to act out their pain to be taken seriously.

Being Harry Potter

*One of the things I could never get accustomed to in my youth
was the difference I found between life and literature.*

JAMES JOYCE

THE PROBLEM WITH STORIES about wizards is
how they make the lives of young readers feel dull
by comparison. A grown-up may rationalize that art is
better than life, but that notion surely has no traction
with children, for whom art is a practical telling of how to
live life. It's hard to remember how we thought about art
before we learned to think of it as optional, or merely an
embellishment of real life. Yet there was a time for all of
us when art conveyed basic knowledge about the world,
and for this, stories are unrivaled. A story unfolds over
time, and there is a largeness in this long unfolding that
evinces authority — the sort of complexity found in real
life. Is it possible to grow up without stories? It's difficult
to imagine other ground so fertile with moral guidance.
Even assuming parents of rectitude, where else does one
learn what is good, kind, and right? These are the essential things to know, whether one wants to fit in, or rebel
against the status quo.

Stories are not, per se, useful only to the well-be-haved. They inflate the gyrations of youth — the whoosh, twist, and scram of various predicaments — with purpose and adventure. Story adventures involve hazards, the unknown, conflict, and occasionally enterprise. As pro-jections of imaginary selves, the stakes become intensely interesting; the potential of stories to mirror the mental life of the reader is made more potent. The truth is, in real life, adventure is rarely encountered. The hazards, unknowables, and conflicts of children's contemporary lives might include deprivation (homelessness, hunger), or danger (crime, substance abuse), but there's never a chance for children to fight evil directly, or find a magical kingdom in the end.

Moral questions contemplated by fictional characters have truck because they are nearly always matters of great consequence. The decisive events of the best stories have the scale and thud of a falling redwood. Children revel in stories because they hint at what exists beyond the veil of the everyday. Stories give away secrets that grown-ups conceal, or confide only begrudgingly. Absorbing plots makes us a more interesting species, and they potentially affirm the gravity and grace of individual actions. Stories also underscore the power of language, arranging words in such a way that they lead to new emotional experiences, and heightened self-awareness. If the intuition of linguists is correct — that an emotion cannot exist without words to name and describe it — then the life trajectories con-veyed in stories also need to be told, so that the complex realities they embody can be felt and imagined by others.

The crux of the issue addressed here is not a shortage of stories, or a lack of interest in them. Luckily, children's stories are abundant, and enjoy a ravenous readership. The first billionaire author in the history of the world, J.K. Rowling, is a writer of books for people mostly between the ages of nine and twelve, although many others have dipped in and become Potter fans. What's less clear, is how to make life more than a wispy simulacrum of the excitement and idealism that stories incite. How can children *be* Harry Potter, rather than merely a follower? The extraordinary passivity that now occupies childhood — a situation which the young have acquired rather than created — makes this contrast an even greater dilemma. It's not that young people aren't busy, it's just that they tend to watch adventure more than they participate in it. But why shouldn't children hope that consequential adventure might inhabit their own lives? Should it only be in fiction that friends can band together, applying courage and ingenuity, if not magic, to defend a small, child-focused universe (for example, school)? Children are hoping for such interesting and important opportunities all of the time, and in that regard, Harry Potter books are less an opportunity for escapism than they are an invitation to consider how interesting life could potentially become.

Subscription to a narrative that pokes at the possibility of an ideal life is not a psychology of childishness, it is the psychology of childhood, and its appeal is quite sensible. When the principal characters in a story acquire special knowledge, and especially when the value of that knowledge is apparent *only* to children, a story affirms the suspicion of young readers that children can be agents of important, socially relevant action. Saving people from despair and evil is appealing work, if you can get it. Not coincidentally, the progenitors of dark plots are often those who rudely condescend to children, or who foolishly underestimate their power, creativity, and grit. The adults in Harry Potter stories may be wise and protecting, but whatever good they propel is separate from, or contingent upon, the goodness and ingenuity of children. To be a child in these stories is to claim an equal share of life's status, an opportunity for ascendant action unfettered by the apprehensions of adults. It should come as no surprise that so many of these young protagonists are cast as orphans.

Literacy is the most obvious benefit of reading, but the best children's literature is also a template for an engaged and active life. The point of stories is not that they put you to bed, but that they wake you up. The cathartic center of children's literature is an invitation for projection, an imagined inhabitation of another place, a different set of circumstances. Literature that elicits such a strong response makes the divide between personal reality and story traversable; a reader is free to skip back and forth between fact and fiction, with each informing the other. We bring our experience to bear on a story, and for children, stories inform a sense of what could be: what is ideal. It's a tumble into imagination, signaling the freedom to believe things for which there is no evidence. This is a freedom still granted to the youngest members of society, for whom there is still sufficient hope that art will influence life. In that sense, fiction is even more transcendent when there is sufficient plausibility, and compelling reasons to identify with a story's principal characters. To be clear, children are identifying not only what they recognize as resembling themselves and their own lives, but what they recognize as ideal, which is for them its own category of truth and guidance.

Inside children's fiction are possibilities for a life enriched by risk and discovery. Yet rarely is risk undertaken gratuitously. Typically, it is required by circumstance, and thus tests tenacity and moral fortitude. Fictional risk leads both characters and readers back to themselves to reflect on personal virtues like courage, ingenuity, and friendship. Here lies the catharsis, because these attributes have infinitely more to do with the *meaning of life for school-age children*, than do school marks, sports, and religion. This contrast is not intended with judgment or denigration. All of the preceding play a definitive role in sculpting a life of purpose. Yet there's an emotional and existential need for children to assimilate myths and stories as a counterbalance to childhood's mounting obligations, inertia, and electronic fatigue. In this thought experiment, I ask that we imagine childhood being formed by personal narrative, a story of a child's own doing, and how those actions might affect personal momentum and lead to self-knowledge.

~

We are a society mired in conflict about the benefits and liabilities of innocence. We panic that children have no time left to be children, and yet demand performance

from them as soon as they begin school, worrying inces-
santly when they are slow to respond. Our ideal child is
someone whose mind seems to work via remote control,
switching between channels for performance and play,
as befits the situation. Contradictory desires cause many
parents, and particularly mothers, to live on the edge,
always anxious about what's being lost because of what's
being gained. Despite this tumult, some beliefs remain
steady. Among these beliefs is that stories are good for
children, in part because they are a non-electronic source
of captivation. That's a relief. But is such captivation
destined for isolation, to be triggered only by what is
fictional and contrived? Can we learn from children's
literature that a sense of agency is a non-negotiable need
of growing up strong?

Great stories use the plausible to leverage belief in
what's *less* believable. As readers, we accept those conditions as the basic parameters of a tale. By contrast, the
abyss between the richness of literature, and the often
impoverished narratives that drive children's lives, is a
global crisis. In the mindscape of childhood, there is a
colossal deficit of attention to what is most important,
and indeed indispensable to youth. This non-negotiable
priority is an opportunity to participate in making the
world. It's an instinct that shows up early on. It is evoked,
for example, by a toddler's will to topple a column of
blocks. That impulse flirts with healthy grandiosity, "I
can make things happen. I can alter the shape of the
physical world. My actions matter." There's less fixity
in a child's perception of reality; they feel that in some

important way the world has begun with them, and that it exists to be affected and changed by "me." In the jargon of psychology this is called egocentrism, but that's a term which barely conceals contempt for the extreme self-interest of children, particularly the unsuppressed desire to have a say in priorities, and how rules are constructed. The popularity of stories flows from an affirmation of this right, and the ways in which stories illustrate how to claim that inheritance.

∾

An instinct to compare oneself to others is as common among children as it is among adults, and the effects are just as serious. To name only a few: an epidemic of existential depression (masked by medications, but never adequately resolved), self-defeating avoidance of reality through substance abuse, and an inability to care seriously about anything beyond one's status and personal needs. I don't know if comparing oneself with those who are exceptional (in the sense of being notably above average in some important way) is a source of stress to children everywhere. But my own conversations with children of diverse backgrounds suggest there is a critical mass of youth who subject themselves to conscious comparison occasionally, and subconscious comparison almost constantly. A nexus of these comparisons is differences in talent, something about which children have little control, but which is nonetheless psychologically segregating. Talented children, on whole, comprise an elite group that get more "air-time," and positive attention. It's a source of tension for those whose talents are less obvious, and who may fixate on how to escape the shadows of more gifted peers or siblings.

It's a conflict that also explains the transformative promise of children's fantasy literature; average kids transcend their normalcy by acquiring extraordinary abilities, and are then needed by others to perform deeds of great importance. Not only is this plot consoling, it illustrates the tendency of children to fantasize about compensating for perceived deficiencies by accomplishing something of substantial merit; something which leads to public recognition, and an acknowledgment of unique abilities. It's hard to feel like you matter if you're only "average." Many young people have been raised in societies where the status of fame has been separated from the work invested in bringing it about. Along with being a distortion of facts, it's a misperception that fails to acknowledge the pleasure of a sustained, goal-directed effort. As this distortion is allowed to flourish, society affirms the cult of fame, and the surrealism of growing up in a world where riches and notoriety are everywhere, but beyond personal reach. For many young people, it feels like a game of chance. Rather than pinning happiness to a well crafted and executed plan, we think like game show contestants: let's spin the wheel and see what we get.

Childhood and parenting practices are under intense scrutiny, but we seem to resist complex explanations for our concerns. Mostly, I think, because we're tired and short of time. There's virtually no forum to discuss or examine the deeper disconnect affecting contemporary youth, which in my view is a lack of synchrony between personal ideals and available choices. It's an epidemic more widespread than ADHD, and it's howling for a cure. Specifically, in what ways can real life better reflect the sense of agency and participation sought by children? Stories spark excitement, but that exhilaration is by definition an act of imagination. If J.K. Rowling and peers have posed a significant challenge to childhood, it's the dilemma of occupying childhood with chronicles of fantastic adventure that have no parallel in real life. Parallels would not require wizardry, but do demand an adjustment of scale, and a viable chance to leave one's imprint on the world. They might require, for instance, a chance to pit oneself against a worthy adversary, other than those on the opposing soccer team, or a zealously strict teacher. When a trio of teens in British Columbia recently dressed as superheroes, and set out to snare sexual predators,[1] they affirmed the powerful lure of doing something unambiguously good, in an unordinary way.

Leaving one's imprint might also include the chance to do something that matters enough to warrant positive public reaction. In my community, I've noticed young people hauling the lumber needed to construct a boardwalk path from a village center into the adjoining forest. Despite my plain description, it's actually a rather monumental task, carefully crafted to traverse wetlands. Being part of this effort is psychologically elevating. It transcends lifting and carrying. It's hard, interesting work, and a focus of community discussion. The path is eagerly anticipated by locals as a means of communing with nature, getting exercise, and allowing wheelchair access to the deep woods. For the eleven- and twelve-year-olds donating their time to this effort, the fun and meaning of the task is the physicality of hauling lumber, the need to move a considerable mass from one space to another, and the sense of building something that is large, and which will be admired by others. It's an unlikely plot for a Harry Potter book, but I doubt it's a task Harry or Hermione would oppose.

Young people need to be admired for accomplishing what is selfless, and credibly good. Yet it strikes me that such opportunities are scarce, if they exist at all in modern childhood. Selling cookies door-to-door, or pledging sponsors for a walkathon have their purposes, but they don't seem sufficiently interesting. Such activities enlist young people as workers, but not as deciders or innovators. Would such activities captivate Harry Potter and friends? I doubt it. Harry seems to be more intrepid than altruistic. Mere altruism is for muggles.

The seriousness of children is diminished by the notion that childhood is a time of passage. And although this is literally true, the same could be said of any other phase of life. The effect of this bias is intense anticipation of the future, and the implication that there are better, or at least more important, things to come. The subjective experience of childhood, however, stands in stark opposition to this conception. It's beautifully captured by William Deresiewicz, in his review of Julian Barnes's *The Sense of an Ending*. Deresiewicz extols Barnes's ability to evoke childhood with "delicacy and reticence... mystery, but also the vivid immediacy, the sense that there is no place and no time but now."[2] The emotive, visual force of "immediacy" deviates from the notion of childhood as a time to focus on preparing for adult success. That preoccupation is symptomatic of a culture built on the pursuit of a "dream," rather than what is "here and now." Americans, especially, seem intent on running from the present, toward an elusive better life. Ralph Waldo Emerson lamented, "We are always getting ready to live, but never living."[3] And Wendell Berry suggests, "The modern mind longs for the future as the medieval mind longed for Heaven. The great aim of modern life has been to improve the future — or even just to reach the future, assuming that the future will inevitably be better."[4] It's the type of feeling we're all aware of, but which evades solution because we are apparently too busy preparing. For what? Primarily, economic ascendance, or more particularly, defending against what might occur in its absence. For others, it's fifteen minutes of promised fame, which is starting to sound like an eternity.

～

Adulthood's harshness has convinced many of us that if childhood isn't effectively managed, children will be lost to idleness or malfeasance. There is some validity to this concern, but the real solution lies in making childhood more about the present than the future. It requires that we give childhood more vivid, narrative power. The gist of this conviction is quite basic: childhood should be, on average, a whole lot more interesting, including a progression of coherent, focused experiences that increase self-knowledge, and which hint at a person's calling. Among other things, childhood demands more hands-on opportunity to achieve an appreciable, visible outcome — something that affects the lives of other people. Living vicariously falls far short of the mark.

Children live in the present, where the transformative experiences they hope for stem from a desire to be an exceptional person, rather than an exceptional pre-adult. A childhood relentlessly focused on preparation reflects anxiety. It's frosty and interferes with the budding of selfhood. The problem is amplified if that preparation (unlike the future "warrior" meme of children's literature) does not involve ninjas, magic, or spy training, but only the brass ring of admission to a prestigious university, or some other indication one has met adult expectations. Stories serve as a useful counterpoint to a psychology of preparation, but are still woefully inadequate in stimulating the plodding momentum of real life.

Getting any traction for this concern is difficult because the response it calls for is less formulaic than, say, aspiring to academic excellence. The prospective benefits of academic excellence are more certain to us, and they're hard to refute. Who doesn't want to see a child or student go to a top university, and achieve economic security? But children themselves hunger for less formulaic experiences. The craving is so great that many now look to schools to sanction and provide the sort of non-academic activities they need to become complete people. At the end of the school day, the experiences that linger may have less to do with the consolidation of important facts than opportunities to be of practical help to a teacher, principal, or another student — in essence, to be an agent of a purposeful outcome.

A child who has helped distribute learning materials, picked up equipment after gym, tended a school garden, made an announcement on the public address system, updated a school website, tutored another student, recommended acquisitions for the library, set up chairs for a school assembly, advocated for a disabled peer or — to share a milestone of my own school days — carefully counted and delivered milk, on a wooden flatbed dolly that has to be tugged down corridors and into classrooms with considerable effort, has had an excellent day.

Any form of agency is better than none, and those that allow a child to make decisions, and require pushing up against the limits of personal capability are the most interesting, and the best loved. One reason so many children want to be chosen to do a job in school is that classrooms are inherently social places where one's status is measured by responsibility and expertise. The teacher's status is clearly greatest, but everyone else wants a taste of that status as well — a job that approximates the importance of the teacher.

The essence here is that childhood needs less waiting and more doing. Whatever progress our societies can claim, these developments have generally excluded children from the possibility of making independent decisions, and from the pleasure of being useful to something or someone else. In fact, we've accomplished just the opposite; children are more dependent and passive than at any time in history. It's not considered safe for many to play outdoors, especially alone, and so play has increasingly become organized by adults, or moved indoors where screens abound with riveting programming. It's hard to blame a ten-year-old for being fascinated with fifteen hundred channels of digital television, or games that spark new sensory plateaus. "He's doing his thing. She likes it." It's hard for everyone to think outside of these mesmerizing boxes.

~

Referring to what is "essential" to childhood is problematic because it ignores what lies beyond the essentials — those things that make childhood ideal. In this way, pragmatism may make us reticent to entertain those ideals. We can become stuck on being realistic at all costs. Idealism, as an aspiration, is a risky assertion to make. Reference to an "ideal" life, even with respect to children, could be interpreted as elitist, or peripheral to "real" problems. A soft economy has a way of making any sort of idealism suspect, perhaps even radical.

Yet no context, no matter how dire, nullifies the basic ecology of childhood, including the benefits of the brain's quest for persistent, and varied stimulation. For example, the hormonal advantages of a more adventurous life, alone, are quite substantial. The adrenal response triggered by absorbing activities can propel greater effort and accomplishment. Basically, when strong, positive emotions are attached to a task, it becomes easier, and more enjoyable. This is true not only for activities involving sports or the arts, but applies to the tedious and repetitive as well, such as taking an IQ test. It's an uncomfortable thought given the prospective consequences, but a child's IQ can vary considerably according to the energy and mood of the person giving the test. Every request to perform is a kind of emotional transaction, and the way the request is made will have some bearing on effort. We may believe that children will put forth their best effort out of deference, but that assumption marginalizes the effect of the attitude and energy adults bring to performance situations — their ability to translate the emotive essence of a task into words and nonverbal exchange. This is the critical capability of transformational parents, teachers, and coaches. Positive emotions are infectious, and they affect the meaning of an experience.

Increasingly, my work with children and their families includes the question, "What sort of experience — typically, some mode of 'doing' — would help this child step outside of an ordinary routine?" It's the feeling of "ordinariness" that is the "blah" standing between what is, and what is ideal. Getting across that divide is the difference between bringing people into the here and now — helping them to see personal relevance — and remaining stuck, skeptical, and uncommitted. In my own experience, and perhaps because of my own emphatic belief, enabling a child to undertake significant actions always enhances traditional talk-based therapies.

The ecology of childhood includes new perspectives of balance which provide striking generational contrasts. For instance, when it comes to the preferred activities of contemporary children, moderation seems antiquated. Consider that the traditional notion of a "hobby," as a hand-based activity someone does in leisure time, is entirely out-of-sync with 21st century youth. The things a young person now does with free time are much more likely to involve electronics, either in the interest of simulated competition, or for instant and continuous communication. For many, "hobbies" are now games which compel something akin to a second life — an avatar that encourages immersion in alternate realities. Although games (or literature) might briefly quell the longing for adventure, there is a major difference between imagining oneself accomplishing extraordinary things, and actually doing so.

At present, adventure tends to signify a degree of "otherworldness," a kind of exceptional life experience to be choreographed by an "adventure expert," or at least a specialized summer camp. Notably, the attributes of adventure, as suggested by games, theme parks, film, and literature, tend to emphasize vicarious and imaginary experience. But a different perspective of adventure might emphasize a journey that takes a person to a deeper understanding of self. This journey would also emphasize being a participant, an agent of action that helps to make an activity resonate because of the seriousness one brings to that task. As a practical matter, adventure can emphasize the transformation of daily activities, and especially those tasks which might be thought of as purposeful work.

In advocating for the young to do purposeful work I don't mean the sort of child labor associated with the nineteenth century. This is not a call for children to be used in crude labor as a means of lifting themselves up economically, or because such labor is perceived to somehow have a beneficial effect on character. The suggestion by former presidential candidate Newt Gingrich that poor, inner-city children should be enlisted as janitors is not an advocation of childhood, but rather an assertion that poverty should be cured by humility and hard work. One wonders if Gingrich is indeed blind to the fine line between humility and humiliation. It's the spirit with which work is undertaken that shapes its meaning. If we go with the Gingrich plan, I favor the idea that the janitorial work of all schools be done by all students, regardless of academic or socioeconomic status. I'm quite confident there would be an ample number of interested students. Cleaning floors and bathrooms would make the day more interesting for many, and would reinforce the caretaking of school buildings as an element of community pride. No money would need to be exchanged — and the rationale for such a requirement would need to be explained to parents. Children, on the other hand, would quickly grasp the logic of the situation, and join its momentum.

Along these lines, Booker T. Washington described the spirit of immersion and agency achieved by the Tuskegee Normal School more than a century ago:

> When a building is to be erected, the teacher in charge of the mechanical and architectural drawing department gives to the class in drawing a

general description of the building desired, and then there is a competition to see whose plan will be accepted. These same students in most cases help do the practical work of putting up the building — some at the sawmill, the brick-yard, or in the carpentry, brickmaking, plastering, painting, and tinsmithing departments. At the same time, care is taken to see not only that the building goes up properly, but that the students, who are under intelligent instructors in their special branch, are taught at the same time the principles, as well as the practical part of the trade. The school has the building in the end, and the students have the knowledge of the trade.[5]

The students who would embrace these tasks far outnumber those who would not. Schools must find ways to recreate this sort of immersion. The self awareness to be gained is far too precious, and time is of the essence.

In some instances, adventure and consequence are found in testing one's expertise, and applying persistence in solving a difficult, important problem. Such was the case for students at fifty schools in Ontario who were enlisted to walk through their respective schools and identify potential obstacles to learning for students disabled by vision, hearing or mobility problems. Jayne Pivik, a professor at the University of Ottawa, was interested in how the sensitivity of children would compare with the perceptual skills of school principals and special education teachers. In all cases, students outperformed adults in spotting learning barriers,[6] with Pivik astutely noting that architects and designers would be well served to consult students before concluding they have addressed all relevant decisions. Studies of this nature further underscore how some categories of knowledge and insight are unique to youth, rather than being the result of accumulated experience. I can't help but imagine that a high school nutrition class, charged with improving school lunches within the existing budget, would manage the task effectively. In this era of market research, why don't we ever ask students how to run schools, or simply involve them directly? Are we just too afraid to discover what they would say?

~

Much of what children learn is factual, explicit knowledge. But the prize of childhood is the tacit knowledge derived from more idiosyncratic, and unplanned learning. Through this rolling mass of experience a person's life assumes a narrative arc, with beginning, middle, and end. The effect of this arc is to join the present moment with the past and future. A narrative distills continuity, and heightens the meaning of significant experiences. This is, for example, why a family disruption such as divorce is a disorienting experience for children; past and future are torn apart, leaving a chasm of discontinuity that at least temporarily changes the meaning of one's life. Of course a person who is subject to such fragmentation has no less narrative than anyone else, but the script which had taken root, and the story of the future to which it pointed, now needs revision. A child whose life has been infused by agency is more likely to feel the right of authorship. A life grounded by conscious narrative helps insulate a child against existential malaise. It makes the decisions of any given moment less arbitrary. A person's story may underscore the inevitability of change, but also reinforces the idea that life is driven by the accumulated experience of its protagonist.

One way of appreciating the value of narrative is to examine lives where it is absent or impoverished. The effects of this impoverishment can be dramatic, yet disguised as a problem of a different origin. A good example is what's known as "failure to launch," a lack of interest in becoming a full-fledged adult that has become an especially acute liability for many young men. Such individuals may be described as "slackers," in reference to their "live and let live, leave me alone, I'll be in the basement," disposition. These circumstances may describe some who fail to launch, but there is surely more to understanding this inertia. For instance, could this stasis be the result of having lived a life that lacks dimension and suitable interest? By this measure, a failure to launch would be understood as never having been oriented to ascend anywhere. What is the sense of launching if one has not yet formed a flight plan?

The routine benchmarks that now signify the trudge from adolescence to adulthood feel slow, dull, and obligatory. In a world that relentlessly portrays status (power, respect, compensation) as an entitlement, the absence of status feels unfair, or even punitive. It's as though one's status is acquired by age or inheritance, rather than one's actions. These sorts of cognitive distortions are rampant among young people, although rarely named and addressed directly. Embedded within the desire for status is a hope to be seen, among other things, as great of mind, or invincible of body. And the dilemma of this wish is its inherent unlikeliness for the great majority. Rather than igniting spirit, it strands a young person in the doldrums of confusion and unarticulated anger. In the most troubling cases, young people seek refuge in endless hours of electronica. But vicarious experience cannot ameliorate the pain of not having fully lived. I know this is a serious indictment to make of youth, but apropos to the consequences of a life lived on the fly, and without any palpable gravity. Such a situation is not, however, inevitable. Detachment and cynicism are not personality traits, so much as an acquired taste for a passivity; for some, a nihilism of indifference. An absence of agency can make the divide between one's idealized and actual self feel too great to overcome, as if there is no way to negotiate a life that is congruent with that ideal self. Without a narrative arc, life can be maddeningly circular; it may not feel like you are headed anywhere, and so there's no obvious reason to go.

If boys retreat into games and the basement, a precursor of "man caves," girls and young women seem to address their confusion by getting lost in the vortex of perfectionism. This includes the nuances of various relationships, preoccupation with the interpretation of social behavior, appearance, and possessions. For girls negotiating the terms of their identity and network, it's a conspiracy of mutual benefit. By focusing on elements of personal control, one feels less vulnerable to the slings and arrows associated with growing up. But the illusion of this approach is that sufficient purpose can be found in life's adjectives, when the gravity that is needed is in the nouns. Networks, while comforting, are not immutable. Learning to think outside a group and for oneself, the way that the protagonists of children's literature do, helps make that transition.

If the most enlightened minds among us are able to see things just as they are, free of projection and distortion, the great majority live in a universe of reflections and mirage. Childhood and adolescence is a time of many mirrors, and who we see reflected is the culmination of our doing, and the substance of our personal stories. When the time to become an adult finally arrives, it is a child's personal history of doing that will propel transformation. In my view, a life of greater scale would more effectively meet the emotional and practical needs of contemporary children. Let me add that these benefits also enable a child to more deeply attach to, and love, other people. Harry Potter teaches children that their actions do matter, and how to make the world bend, if ever so slightly, to the contours of this emerging self. Enlarging life's scale, then, is no less than carving a place to exist in the world, making oneself at home here.

School as Wisdom Culture

I

THE PURPOSE OF GOING TO SCHOOL is unnecessarily limited. It has been made so by passive agreement to narrow the meaning of K–12 education, and by disregard for its prospective contribution to a more reflective and satisfying life. This is a collusion between those who govern education's form and content — what is taught, and how — and those who pay for education. As societies, we do not speak openly of this agreement because the basis of the partnership is self-evident; economic and social ascendance for many, and continued prosperity for those already on track. There is little to be gained from arguing against a desire for ascendance; the benefits of economic security are too obvious. But to pursue such strength in a vacuum is equally nonsensical. We cannot hope to educate the next generation for the good life without making a more considered life part of that equation. Schools are an essential catalyst for this growth, and for shaping people whose strength should be manifest more in their citizenship than consumption.

Education tends to inspire passionate debate because the stakes are high, and the consequences of failure, serious. In discussing "failure," we tend to focus on disengaged students willing to let the prize of education slip through their fingers. It's an attitude that strikes us as tragic, and which is openly defiant of education's promise to bolster economic safety. In the United States, much is made of public education's demise; it is both a practical matter, and an issue of national esteem. Dialogue obsessively dissects the bottom third of school performers, where many do not finish high school. In the most troubled districts, schools and students are indicted for a conspiracy to fail. It is said that students are not working hard enough, or at all, and that schools are not doing enough to motivate them, or hold students accountable.

But is such an effort a reasonable expectation in an atmosphere of reduced relevance; a context in which the meaning of life now, and the relevance of education to life in the future, remains unnecessarily obscure? Those young people who successfully hurtle their way through school oblivious to this reduction demonstrate that willpower and discipline can overcome doubt (if not poverty), but is this a suitable model for the "exemplary student?" Can we locate within our own character and calling an intuition that societies of learned people and great literature should be able to provide a more transcendent education? It does not seem so. Evidence suggests we are more committed to working harder at the same approach, and the effect is an increasing divide between educational haves, and have-nots.

Nearly all students are affected by education's tendency to refer back to itself, because that is the nature of textbooks and packaged curricula, which cannot practically address the circumstances of individual learners. Textbooks obstruct engagement not only by standardizing content, but also by marginalizing the life one brings to school. Not only is such a system pernicious and circular, it is anti-wisdom, and thus invalidating of education's larger purpose. There is little hope of elucidating one's role in civilization by reading from a standard text. We should be grateful for teachers gifted in an ability to reach beyond these texts, but we should be even more adamant that the content of education be sufficiently diverse, and capable of incorporating the idiosyncratic interests of individual learners.

In a vast literature of education's needs, wisdom barely rates a mention. Perhaps because it seems too abstract, its acquisition more a function of personal differences than educational excellence. Wisdom is a more social phenomenon than intelligence. Its relevance touches everyone, and its pleasures are unbiased by social status. More to the point, the pursuit of wisdom makes going to school exponentially more interesting. Students, however, do not know that. Most think wisdom is antique, the stuff old people aspire to, and which has no bearing on youth. It is true that wisdom becomes more dense and satisfying with age, but that does not preclude a role for wisdom in youth. There is no evidence that young people are uninterested in defining a moral code for their lives, or for developing the skills of personal inquiry. I suggest that they have a nearly insatiable appetite for this discourse, and are waiting for educational leaders to notice. That being said, those who presume to impart wisdom will need a different, youth-centric idea of what wisdom means. This reconfiguration of wisdom is at the center of building a wisdom culture.

It's satisfying to acquire wisdom, but frustrating when gained too late to be applied to formative situations defining the trajectory and purpose of one's life. Education — by which I mean the whole of those activities which take place at school, or on behalf of school — is increasingly peripheral to the spirit of childhood. The battles waged over education's form and content are mostly about grades, which say little about a person's journey toward self-knowledge. Owing to the great economic anxieties of our time, the learning and behavioral attributes of children have come under intense examination. This compartmentalization of childhood has prompted the pursuit of abilities, rather than the cultivation of complete persons, and a sense of personal significance.

Thus the purpose of going to school is driven less by a philosophy — a perspective requiring reasoned reflection and moral action — than by a rationale. The prevailing rationale is that education provides a good return on investment. Where some may pay substantial sums for a more privileged education, the expected return is accordingly swollen. For the majority of children, expectations are more modest, yet a common formulation applies: one's tax dollars or tuition ought to be translated into preparation for gainful employment. Whether or not an individual actually becomes educated is a secondary concern. There is a genuine desire to alleviate poverty, and to position economically disadvantaged students for decent jobs. But growing up in poverty should not doom one to a superficial, impoverished discussion about the role of school in her or his life. A "job" is a less complete idea than the notion of vocation. Children from poor families have as much interest and need in understanding their significance as those whose lives are propelled by wealth.

School unfolds not only the meaning of events and facts, but also one's personhood. In our time, where information has become so accessible as to seem mundane, self-understanding may be the most important body of knowledge to be gained by going to school. This is more than personality traits and opinions. It is the shape of one's existential orbit, the roles one might play within the world now, and in adulthood. And although students repeatedly ask themselves these questions, there is little or no facilitated dialogue. It is a missed opportunity of great consequence, because going to school is not a dress rehearsal. We are changed by school; it gives us an opportunity to push up against the parameters of our preconceptions, and test alternative narratives about who we are, and what matters. This should not be the privilege of an elite few, lucky enough to be educated by teachers who see the symbiosis of school and civilization. It should be the basic reflex of school, an initiation into the full force of citizenship.

Education is a magnet for public attention. It is sensible to seek justification for an activity that demands so many hours of the day, across so many years. No waking activity comes close to requiring as much time as school during the first third of life. That the intent and value of such an arduous endeavor should come under close scrutiny is to be expected. Yet the long history of education's critique rarely, if ever, focuses upon why one should go to school in the first place. Instead, it gnaws away ad infinitum at the systemic failures that are all too easy to spot: is a particular school producing enough students with passing grades? Are teachers working hard enough? Do they really care? Are sufficient numbers of students planning to attend college? With such an approach, we presume to measure a universe with calipers.

Beyond these basic concerns is the major subtextual question which, although unarticulated, continues to govern societal judgment about education: is this community consistently producing economically viable consumers? In the absence of any other articulated objective, the purpose of education is to provide continued economic security. In this sense, school is primarily a means of leveraging a desirable outcome, largely divested of any serious consideration about personhood, or the vocational enrichment of young people. Used here, vocation refers to the fulfillment of a person's calling — a more complex and personal idea than the notion of job or career. This is particularly true in public schools, where actions that hint at passion, personality, or deviation from the norm, must fly under the radar to avoid community demagogues or opportunistic litigation. Today, many communities have vocal members, professionally enraged with education. The push for privatizing public schooling has empowered an army of social sharpshooters, quick to spot potential platforms for politicizing school. It should not surprise us that the average American public school cowers under a cloak of blandness.

Thus the prevailing assumptions of education, whether unconscious or merely unspoken, preclude a serious relationship with an ethos of learning that aspires to make school a *wisdom culture* — a learning community in which knowledge is neither a commodity to be traded, nor something so abstract as to become self-referential. In a wisdom culture, knowledge is inherently useful, and built from diverse ways of knowing, and equally varied learning experiences. There is no hierarchy of knowing within a wisdom culture that subordinates the manual to the intellectual. Doing is not less than thinking, yet both doing and thinking are made responsible to a larger, more complex understanding of life's purpose. Unraveling that constellation of purpose is education's ultimate possibility. This is a concept of wisdom that speaks to youth by virtue of its immediate relevance, and because the true subject of wisdom is people rather than information. We are less in need of any further rationale for developing wisdom cultures, than we are in need of a war on venality, ignorance, and the inane.

≈

There seem to be several reasons that people continue to go to secondary school beyond feeling obligated to do as told. None of these reasons has much to do with becoming well educated. First, and most dominant, is the matter of economic aspiration. Many people go to school, or send their children, in hope of securing basic qualifications for a "good job," or at least a better job than they might get otherwise. Second are those who also go to school with money on their mind, but rather than aspiring to an above average level of comfort, simply hope to avoid economic hardship. Such individuals often circulate among the bottom half of school performers, doing just enough to stave off the disaster of school failure, and the bleak possibility of perpetual unemployment. There is a third group for whom school is a much more social enterprise, rather like a party with its own economy of values such as attractiveness, likability, status, and influence. The fourth group of students are those who are psychically and spiritually lost. Despite, or perhaps because of that disorientation, they find the structure of the school day vaguely reassuring. Having assessed the possibilities, these students conclude that going to school provides at least some shelter from the anxiety of a directionless future. This is a kind of suspended reality — a belief that physically going to school is the same as becoming educated.

In every case, school is being used to either achieve or avoid something, but not necessarily to participate in something. What makes this proximal distinction significant is that becoming educated exists outside of these parameters. Specifically, becoming educated — participating in a wisdom culture — is not about *achieving* anything in particular. One might speak of achieving a well-informed mind, or achieving some capacity for citizenship, but those accomplishments are not planned in the same way that one plans to become a scientist, attorney, or musician. Among even the intellectually inclined, such achievements are almost always reserved for post-secondary students, who themselves may come under fire for educational tangents without apparent connection to career prospects.

If there is a prominent sign of secondary and post secondary education's failure to clarify its purpose, it is evident in various forms of truancy. Basic truancy involves skipping school, but other kinds of truancy reflect more complex attitudes, and may ultimately have more serious consequences. Failing to continue with school after high school is a kind of truancy that has adversely affected boys in particular. Young men are increasingly less likely to attend a university, or even give it much consideration. The essence of this crisis is not that young men cannot get admitted to higher education; it's that they see little value in the endeavor. Those concerned by this argue that boys no longer view college as a sound financial investment, or that the slow, regimented pace of going to school is not agreeable to boys. There is surely some truth in these insights, but the larger issue affecting young men is that school forces them to separate abilities, interests, and ideals in such a way that their selves are fragmented, and forced into conflict. The best way for school to appeal to these students, and others who are increasingly inclined to look for personal relevance outside of school, is to construct new narratives about what school is for. A school-based wisdom culture would be prepared to do just that using conversation, literature, and personal experience as conduits for those narratives. That commitment, by itself, promises to immediately make school more compelling. In this way, a wisdom culture makes it less interesting or cool to be truant.

The enemies of wisdom culture are both systemic and electronic. In some quarters, the numbing effects of the latter are enabled by sheer prevalence: electronica has found an ideal host in the human sensorium. Stimulation is literally on everyone's mind, and there are few barriers to accessing electronica at school. Electronica is exceptionally good at concealing itself — as though it knows it's doing something wrong. And indeed there is some question as to whether electronica is received by youth as a utopian ideal, or as a viral, dystopian condition in which the invasiveness of stimulation has overwhelmed all human defenses. Think fast: do gadgets and games better stir tension and irritability, or promote contentment and euphoria?

In an essay on Nadine Gordimer (and in defense of literature), Susan Sontag declares, "Everybody in our debauched culture invites us to *simplify* reality, to *despise* wisdom."[1] This is a serious accusation, implying a degree of volition, and an ideology which if not anti-intellectual, is at least averse to complexity. Those conditions may indeed exist, but I believe there is hope as well, because I've seen no such attitude among students in middle and secondary school. To the contrary, just the opposite — people with an intense interest in serious conversation. Neither wisdom nor its pursuit is typically associated with middle school age students, but the reason for this blindness is that the formative conditions of middle school make little allowance for wisdom culture. There is no sustained forum in which the deeper concerns of students might emerge, and be met with serious regard. But the nascent capacity is there, even though interest in wisdom gets drowned out by the vacuous cacophony of distraction that bombards young minds daily. The difficulty then is not an absence of will, or a lack of desire for personally meaningful dialogue. The principal burden is one of interference. Specifically, the unrelenting, emotive sounds that buzz adolescent ears. The omnipresent concert of music, rings, beeps, and banter that syncopate adolescent life may be the most obvious, yet least discussed, element of generational divide in the world today. It is a different perceptual reality that has moved thinking about the future — planning — to the edges of one's life map.

Grappling with one's purpose and perspectives is inherently difficult. It requires persistent, focused thought. A wisdom culture seeks to transcend the loop of electronica in the interest of encouraging more active participation in the construction of knowledge. It requires analysis, reason, deduction, and debate — beyond listening and reading. And it's essential for such an effort to be made early, and sustained throughout middle and secondary school. Intellectual interest that finds no culture of wisdom at those optimal moments will remain constrained within mono-loops of stimulation, destined for atrophy like any ignored muscle.

Technology has improved many aspects of the human condition, but it has had a more lateral effect on knowledge acquisition. The electronic dissemination of facts, for example, enables rapid assimilation, but may also encourage premature conclusions to complex questions. As technology binds opinion with fact at nanospeed, it becomes harder to sort out the difference. During this cognitive-cultural transition, when we ostensibly need more time to map content, we are inclined to take much less. There is, in effect, no gestation period during which a person can sort out ideas and truth, placing them in a context of existing knowledge. Added to this liability is the alienation engendered from living among a profusion of facts, with little opportunity to act on specifics, or to effect any sort of material response. Generally, students are sequestered in smallish rooms where the consolidation of abundant information is of paramount importance. The best teachers help students to get beyond this anxiety, but the system itself is rigged to heighten self-consciousness and comparison. If such circumstances are not considered pathological, it is only because they are so common that the afflicted outnumber the well. It's precisely this sort of imbalance that makes the pursuit of wisdom seem archaic, rigid, or blithely self-important. This, even as wisdom has few outspoken advocates, and no political heft. The systemic threats to wisdom culture pivot around the slow creep toward a debased pragmatism. This perspective makes little connection with more humanistic ideals of innovation and self-reliance, and instead is reductive, fearful, and dominated by a psychology of scarcity. Advocacy of wisdom seems unfortunately fated to incite reactions of "extraneous" or "expensive," even where it might involve only an element of personal agency.

Despite encumbrance and adversity, however, the assimilation of wisdom remains viable. Neither electronic barriers to focus, nor the difficulty of cultivating an explicit appreciation of wisdom, are the same as an absence of interest in deep thinking. Particularly where the key subject of inquiry is oneself, the interest in wisdom culture is intensified. Conversely, the exclusion of selfhood signals a less emotional and less interesting conception of wisdom. In the world of adolescence, what is not personal tends to be received as dull and peripheral. This is not self-absorption; it is the nature of life in the western world, for a handful of turbulent years.

Because the education of youth has become unbalanced, favoring an intake of content over a plan of action, young people are searching for a sense of agency, and they intuitively sense it cannot be found without first looking inward. The conflict is further complicated by those who would purport to lead, but for whom wisdom is simply not on the radar. An effective school-based wisdom culture is not fixated on traditional notions of scholarship as much as it is on nurturing a passion for knowledge and hybrid modes of inquiry. This is a challenge that demands serious consideration, and which invites schools to assume greater leadership in constructing an education relevant to a civilization of diverse people, each hoping to know their own significance.

≈

Caring for children begins with love and the provision of basic needs, including protection of their physical and emotional selves. Adult instincts about how to protect children say much about how we imagine childhood, especially the association made between innocence and a good childhood. Yet in protecting children too stridently, we may shield not only individuals, but childhood itself, from an opportunity for elevation. The word "child," even when used to designate relationship rather than age, implies someone less fully formed, and in that regard, less complex. The will to protect children certifies our belief in the determinism of youth, the idea that we can't escape the destiny written by our earliest days. But the spiritual needs of human beings — including those of children — are easily obscured by good intentions.

The state to which childhood aspires is less one of protection than *agency*: those individual actions which garner recognition and approval for the character and skill they demonstrate. The most basic forms of agency stem from the resolution of practical problems, while more advanced forms blossom from having made oneself important, relevant to someone or something larger than oneself. Although agency is enriched by skill and knowledge, these alone do not equal agency. Until knowing is animated by an opportunity to do, wisdom remains abstract and elusive. The notion that education is well complemented by an opportunity to act on what one learns is not a new idea. It has substantial roots in the literature of transcendentalism, and especially the writings of Henry David Thoreau:

> The student who secures his coveted leisure and
> retirement by systematically shirking any labor
> necessary to man obtains but an ignoble and un-
> profitable leisure, defrauding himself of the ex-

perience which alone can make leisure fruitful. "But," says one, "you do not mean that students should go to work with their hands instead of their heads?" I do not mean that exactly, but I mean something which he might think a good deal like that; I mean that they should not *play* life, or *study* it merely, while the community supports them at this expensive game, but earnestly *live* it from beginning to end. How could youths better learn to live than by at once trying the experiment of living?[2]

If agency was as rare in Thoreau's time as this passage suggests, the challenges of the present are certainly more daunting. Yet if Thoreau was touching upon an enduring need of youth, one which cannot be ignored without unraveling a young person's tether to the realism of the world, then it is certainly incumbent upon those standing watch now to bring youth to life.

II

A wisdom culture cannot be built by a school that becomes preoccupied with transient trends, or crises that disproportionately consume time and energy. For example, considerable time is spent talking about the evils of bullying, and advocating for victims, but far less time discussing the more pervasive forces that undermine civic life, and which contribute to bullying in the first place. Bullying is,

SCHOOL AS WISDOM CULTURE | 123

of course, indefensible. But it is simplistic to make bullies the meme for the numerous subtle and overt forms of incivility that occur in public life. Within schools, it is more expeditious to hold a topical assembly and hope for the best, than it is to begin a series of smaller community dialogues about stereotypes, impatience, and egotism. The very point of a wisdom culture is to construct a system of learning and reflection that can examine these choices with greater objectivity. Rather than driving bullying behavior underground, or into new forms of antagonism, a wisdom culture works to root it out for the long term, because a robust atmosphere of self-knowledge, agency, and purpose smothers social aggression.

A wisdom culture values intelligence, and the apprehension of complexity as useful and commendable, but not as things to be revered for their own sake. Insular thinking and self-referentialism are anathema to an educational culture that sees itself as a bridge to a larger world. A founding purpose of a wisdom culture would be the will to connect learning with problems and situations that have serious consequences for the human condition. Those challenges are considered with an eye toward the diverse needs of different people, and with an assumption that collaboration is usually required to solve hard problems. Following the spirit of this idea, wisdom might as easily be shared through co-participation in a physical task as by teaching or counsel. Throughout, a wisdom culture is driven less by desire for esoteric knowledge than it is for knowledge about how to live well, and congruent with one's core values. There is no hierarchy of better ways to acquire wisdom, where wisdom is pursued to serve the common good. In a wisdom culture people are more important than talent, brilliance, or scholarship. Yet each of these elements might conceivably serve the common good without conceit.

The moral imperative to create wisdom cultures speaks less to the pursuit of the perfect life than it does to the development of well people. The malaise and confusion of adolescence pivots on a misunderstanding of relationship with the larger world. Young people tend to see themselves as more dynamic than others, and thus feel compelled to make a bold, memorable mark. It's life as graffiti, and the deepest meaning of one's mark is that "I am here. I will not be ignored." To grow up, or become mature, means to see past that false sense of separation and omnipotence. Addressing the gap between the figure of *self* and the ground of *context* is part of acquiring wisdom. A good life doesn't feel plausible until this connection is made; it is an intuition about how to belong, and what one's role should be. Students should experiment with connecting figure to ground while still in school. This is the work of building self-knowledge, and which makes one's calling audible. In my view, and in my work with young people, this is one of youth's most exciting moments. A belief that one's life should be shaped by calling, rather than accident or arbitrary choice, is a powerful conviction for a young person. It is, as well, a powerful mindset for schools.

In conveying that life can be whatever one chooses, adults intend to encourage youth, but this idea is inadvertently confusing, and antithetical to the notion of a calling. The idea that one can do anything imaginable lacks validity to most children, at least by the time they reach age ten. There is no gravity in that idea, because "anything" is vague and diffuse; it is a journey without realism or urgency. In our enthusiasm to affirm possibilities, we may neglect to foster the gifts and inclinations that govern an individual's natural self. Discovering and acting upon these inclinations is as important to happiness and the capacity for civility, as is social competence. A civil society implies not only a sense of adherence to rules and etiquette, but an interest in amicable participation. Civility requires that its adherents have a solid sense of themselves, and school is an ideal place to cultivate this awareness. Nowhere in childhood is there a greater fusion of social experience, and concordant opportunity for its exploration.

The sense of community and nationhood to which modern societies aspire is impossible without the union of figure and ground. This hope must confront the illiberal homogenization encouraged by a burgeoning global marketplace. Community, nationhood, and citizenship are the identities we depend upon to defy the erosion of valued differences. They will not be surrendered without a fight. Even those young people who take cover in life's margins have an investment in their own sovereignty. Consider that simple truancy is a form of passive aggression, spurred by the feeling that one no longer *belongs* at school.

If the need to help young people connect their authentic selves with context is accepted as *a priori*, then the composition of childhood itself can be productively re-examined. For instance, once the paths of selfhood and belonging are understood as interdependent, it makes little sense to think of growing up and going to school as separate things. The significance of school flows most fundamentally from how much time it requires. This massive investment of cognitive effort, coupled with the social intensity of school, makes one's education inseparable from childhood as both concept and experience. Consequently, schools are partners in raising children as much as they are in educating them. That societies have allowed school to steadily encroach upon family time says much about the angst that shapes our collective concerns about childhood. Look no further than families' compliance with the intention of coveted schools to lengthen the school day, and increase the volume of homework. Agreement with such policies signals frustration with not having any other way to reinforce the importance of school. Thus increasing the accountability of school is modeled on contemporary thinking about workday imperatives; work more overtime, take home more work, institute more performance evaluations. And of course teachers are construed as "managers" responsible for the performance of their subordinates — though none get to hire and fire the members of their "team."

It seems as though most societies are still in transition with respect to understanding the enlarged role of school in bringing young people into the world. Traditionally, the activities of childhood have been bifurcated, categorized as belonging to either family or school. Yet the roles of parents and teachers are shifting as the allocation of parenting time within families is diminished. As a result, extracurricular school activities take on greater importance. Is it enough for soccer practice to simply prepare someone to play better soccer? Is math club the most useful supplemental knowledge a student might pursue after regular school hours? What exactly *is* our theory of extracurricular activities, and their contribution to the making of a whole person? Although these questions suggest an increased burden for schools, they also inspire possibilities that branch from being granted such a broad license. Ideally, schools would nurture an inclusive wisdom culture, incorporating parents and community as essential partners. I believe the schools of this century's future will be educational centers for entire families, and in becoming so, will work around the primitive dichotomies of family and school, person and student, that inform conventional perceptions of youth. As families and communities we are already there in spirit and need, but still lack a suitable mechanics for this collaboration.

∾

Progressively-minded educators speak of wanting to create learning communities, grounded in empathy and consideration. My work has enabled me to visit schools that have created an atmosphere of community to which students readily subscribe. And I have witnessed the work of charismatic educational leaders, able to bring people and educational vision together. In most cases, students are eager to align themselves with the paths of tradition provided for them. In the parlance of social psychology, this cohesion is referred to as *field dependence* — a person's actions, and the beliefs that prompt them, are influenced by the *field* (community structure and values) in which one exists. A field-dependent person is responsible to others in the same community, and especially to the traditions and mores that define that community. In this way, many communities governed by religious principles have a high degree of field dependence, as does one driven by a code of honor, such as among soldiers, or a code to "do no harm" as is shared by physicians.

The protocol found in many private schools sets the stage for field dependence. And the same structural tools are now used by some charter and public schools to create an atmosphere of shared values. Overall, this is an important accomplishment, enhancing a sense of belonging for most. Yet having instilled interdependence and community, how does a school convey their meaning beyond a need for order? It's one thing to cultivate an atmosphere in which students are highly identified with each other, and in which they feel compelled to follow a common set of principles. But that is not the same as clarifying what the personal or community value of that journey is for. When Thoreau advises "All men want, not something to *do with*, but something to *do*, or rather something to *be*,"[3] he is addressing the difference between identifying with something, and the need to be a significant member of something. This might also be thought of as the gap between a person's latent interests and capabilities, and the application of those attributes to a more specific identity. It's a tension that shapes the emergence of girls as much as it does boys, and which calls for attention *during* adolescence. No one wants to wait until the age of twenty-five to do important, useful things. This core need cannot be satisfied with mottos or character education. We are in immediate need of mentored possibilities — purposeful work that can accommodate the ideas and emergent maturity of youth. It is such work which gives life an enduring form, and which endows young people with the confidence to accept the onset of adulthood. Accordingly, anxiety about becoming an adult, felt by so many, testifies to a personal history void of transcendent, self-directed vocation.

Now is the time for education to challenge the burgeoning commercial monopoly on the production of meaning. We should not reduce wisdom culture to a set of "outcome measures," or a prefabricated rubric that is neither important, nor offensive to anyone. A wisdom culture is not a commercial enterprise; it needs more gravity than a memorable slogan. The inherent excitement of education has to do with feeling that knowledge is being unfolded for the first time, which of course it is with respect to individual learners. Surely, school is not for the production of functional and compliant citizens with no idea as to what they are subscribing, other than the demands of the economy. In important ways, education is the obvious resistance to this lopsidedness. But in cases, it is unclear where the loyalties of school lie. Let us be cautious to avoid oversimplification: the point is not whether the purpose of education is to serve the interests of the young, or those of a broader society. The premise of wisdom culture is that by seeking to invest young people with a more integrated understanding of the world and themselves, schools move toward the resilience and improvement of societies. They make the world a more livable place.

III

To believe in learning as a noble and cultured proposition may be logical, but that is not the image conjured when most think of education. Here, in the looming shadow of recession, education holds more significance as an antidote to a sagging social safety net, than as a means of acquiring knowledge or sagacity. Becoming a learned person occasionally earns public approval, but that end remains peripheral to the nation's primary demands of education. The most coveted outcome is a synthesis of hope and magical thinking: good grades can be achieved by subpar students. The notion that anything can be achieved via manic, maximal effort informs national incentive programs such as Race to the Top. State commissioners of public education eager for funding and national visibility embrace such programs, and in the process make achievement — as measured almost exclusively by test scores — the purpose of education.

These initiatives appeal to the egalitarian spirit of the public as well, reassuring us that those who do not do well in school can be made to do so with enough ingenuity by school administrators, and an abundance of hard work on the part of teachers. Because good students are already receiving satisfactory grades, they receive much less concern. There is both honesty and naiveté in the will to use test scores as the key measure of whether education is working. It is an obsession that indicates where the drama of school is focused. Many fewer of us are concerned about whether students are sufficiently well educated to read and understand literature, track scientific discoveries, detect confabulation, or decode art.

It is unclear whether a society thus committed can imagine the transformative possibilities of wisdom culture, or if such a culture is sufficiently relevant to pressing social priorities. Incessant focus on outcome has the effect of making school feel as if it is primarily a platform for future success. There is a denial of the present implicit in this attitude. It is as if the experiences of childhood and adolescence were by definition lesser experiences, those which precede the important stuff of life. And because this idea is pervasive, there is a concomitant shift away from the experiential benefits of education, devaluing what it means to go to school and to devote such a large quantity of time to the cultivation of mind.

Most problematic is that any possible interest in wisdom culture is inhibited by the belief that the purpose of education is to be an accelerator of ascendance — upward mobility. And in fact there is little evidence of any meaningful resistance against this intransigence. Yet the pursuit of ascendance and wisdom are not easily compatible.

Self-knowledge implies its own kind of ascendance, one that evolves through insight and synthesis. Rather than a series of *eureka* moments, wisdom tends to be gathered and digested slowly. If this undertaking sounds like the exclusive terrain of scholars absorbed by the esoteric, I ask you to imagine the intensity of a group of fifteen-year-olds debating the idea of destiny, the vigor with which twelve-year-olds discuss the contemporary meaning of heroism, or the way in which a seventeen-year-old challenges the "wisdom" of her parents' beliefs about the purpose of college. These are but a few examples of an eagerness to deconstruct the beliefs and assumptions that bind societies together, and tear them apart. When that membrane becomes visible, and is made available for examination — both benign and adversarial — learning moves at the speed of light. No one wants the experience to end. These are the moments of critical difference. Yet questions like "Who are we? What should we do?" are not often asked in schools, because no one designed and approved the accompanying textbook.

There is no shortage of community anger at what schools don't accomplish. But I have wondered if the ire of communities simply reflects the resentment of a society in which most have been denied a life that feels adequately meaningful and interesting? Underneath the feeling is a belief that one has not been sufficiently cared for. It stands to reason that such an awareness would lead to discontentment. When parents campaign for their children to be well educated, they are asserting their right to some power over their children's fate. School officials are equally desirous of meaningful power and influence. But consider what happens to a principal who tries to influence the pedagogy of her or his school. Any type of teaching practice considered nontraditional is likely to be challenged. There would certainly be reaction to the teaching of content considered irrelevant to primary outcome measures. Where is the possibility of creative leadership within such an institution, and how does this constriction affect the psyche of those charged with overseeing the atmosphere of a school? Arguably, the fact that so many school principals have become invested in cultivating a climate of discipline indicates the depth of their frustration. The one area left to school leaders to make their mark is the arena of discipline. Almost everybody approves of well behaved students.

The depth of our collective grief about the devolving purpose of education is exemplified in our anticipation that games are a probable template for the future of schooling. Although many disbelieve such a transformation is for the best, the powerful insurgence of games — and their psychology — has made them influential, something beyond what "games" should be. Thus our acceptance of games can be construed as a defense mechanism, something along the lines of Freud's *reaction formation*, in which a person subconsciously chooses to identify with an adversary, rather than contend with the anxiety of being in conflict with that foe. And it's not entirely irrational. There is hope for an education that instills curiosity and rapport, able to command sustained attention. At present, however, this hope may be marked by overemphasis on teaching methods, as compared with the power of content and discretionary time. Specifically, school risks the disengagement of students by way of insisting on the subjugation of attention to prescribed content, which may not easily sync with the interests of diverse learners. An education excessively stiffened by instructional mandates points to a set of priorities that inherently diminishes critical differences among students. Mandates often fail to clarify why it is important to go to school in the first place.

~

If a wisdom culture is to be cultivated, those charged with sustaining its ethos will have to be more than well qualified — they will have to be well cared for. When K–12 education is criticized, commentary usually focuses upon the qualification of teachers, and the techniques by which they should be held accountable. It is an approach marked by aggression more than affection. Some members of the public clamor for teachers to be treated as contracted laborers. Yet it makes little sense to compartmentalize our feelings about teachers from the feelings we have for children — especially our own. Simply stated, the health and well-being of education rests heavily upon the well-being of its providers.

In this regard, there is little hope of improving education without addressing the emotional and intellectual conditions of teaching itself. The notion that the spiritual life of educators is central to the mission of education is radical commonsense. How can teachers conceivably create an atmosphere that is the nexus of great education, unless or until they feel identified with the purpose of their work? Surely not all teachers come to the practice of teaching with an explicit interest in the meaning of their vocation. But I believe most look beyond the reductive notion of teaching excellence as defined by students' grades. Young people should be invited to opine on this topic, because that is the best way to encourage their own moral consciousness, and to make them partners in the goal of educational excellence. Through such a dialogue, teaching's scope of interest is broadened, and teaching is elevated from professional obligation to craft. One should not even ponder the possibility of a career in education without an aspiration to craft something beautiful.

Current thinking about teachers indicates how far we have drifted from a humanistic, wisdom-centric perspective of what teaching is, and what it should accomplish. The care of teachers should directly address the intellectual dimensions of teaching, treating teaching as a wisdom-centric endeavor. Teachers are provided with ample professional education, but most of it addresses either teaching habits, or summarizes research which does little to encourage a passion for the profession. It is dishonest for a society to demand greater performance and outcome (including happy, well-adjusted youth), but be ignorant of the means by which this is achieved. Caring for teachers is not a matter of deference or simplemindedness. It is an acknowledgment of how teaching touches young minds.

When students aspire to be teachers themselves, they are communicating their identification with the ideals of teaching. One's best teachers are an enduring memory; their care is an affirmation, some reassurance that one does not have to face the rigors of school — and growing up — alone. School is a community of many such caretakers, and in the minds of students they exist, like parents, for the benefit of the young. Of course this is an ideal, but for many, it is their first exposure to a life driven by vocation. To be taught by someone whose satisfaction with the task is palpable is comforting and inviting. It seems important for schools to proceed with an intention of living up to that ideal.

In order for wisdom culture to attract enthusiasm it will require leadership in the form of school heads, superintendents, commissioners of education, and school boards. Almost every independent school's mission statement suggests, "We are creating tomorrow's leaders..." But what does this mean at present? We can cultivate leadership to operate within or outside of prevailing values. In either case, it is an effort that encourages responsible citizenship. We need authors of a moral universe, able to script lives congruent with their core values. If this seems utopian, it's a sign we have hit upon a purpose worthy of our status as mentors, and the needs of the next generation. It is during the first decades of life where leadership should gain traction, rescuing it from vague associations with little immediate relevance. School is the temporary fortress where such a discourse is still possible.

If young people have no tangible way to act on their

conscience, or are made to feel that such inclinations are exceptional rather than ordinary, citizenship will be no more than an occasional thought. For example, the frequent conflation of leadership and heroism is confusing. It is symptomatic of a culture which can find no will or way to lead outside of dangerous sacrifice. A key task of a school-based wisdom culture, then, is to frame a broad model of social responsibility, clarifying the relevance of wisdom to various present day circumstances. School is an ideal place for this sort of incubation to occur. In part, because schools benefit from resilience in ways that other social institutions do not, they are given some latitude in policy and procedure, and there is a fundamental "goodness" to what happens at school. That latitude is a small vestige of education's roots, a belief in freedom of mind and its seminal place within scholarship.

Still, schools are not without a history of liability. The infantilizing effects of education can be found in its mandate for discipline and hierarchy, as well as its assumption that students are too young to know their own minds. A wisdom culture seeks to develop presence of mind that is the antithesis of reactivity. It does not hesitate to define the particulars of its mission, and it draws upon the strength of that clarity to help students define themselves. Such a culture does not demand compliance but it does command respect. It recycles that respect as regard for its constituents.

∼

It is customary to rebut the arguments I have made here with concerns about insufficient time and a lack of autonomy. There are legitimate concerns regarding both, which might cause any hope for these ideas to quickly dissolve. Along those lines, wisdom culture needs viable models. And the best way to begin is for schools to construct those models from available resources. This will certainly include school personnel, families, and community ties. I have tried to describe an educational ethos which could be integrated into the day-to-day work of schools, but it would be foolish to think one can anticipate the form a wisdom culture might assume, from one school to the next. To attempt such a recipe would obstruct the very process I am advocating.

It is no longer sufficient to dedicate oneself or one's school to developing intelligent students. Intelligence has no morality. It is not endowed with character, or the will to accomplish anything of significance. Intelligence does not guarantee either a life of interest or fulfillment. Yet a search for personal relevance, aided by literary and practical inquiry, promises to draw from intelligence and imagination a life of one's own making. This is a life in which industry flows from insight, and in which self-knowledge is understood as distinct from self-absorption. The way in which young people participate in a wisdom culture will vary considerably. The imperative of mentors is to validate a persistent effort, employing diverse methods of inquiry. Such an effort requires the vocal approval of school heads, and public dialogue about the ways and means of this humanistic enterprise within a school community.

For many, leadership is now associated with problem-solving. I do not discount the value of solving problems, but the leadership needed to build wisdom cultures is inherently more creative. It needs ingenuity, and the resolve to devise something new. Whatever shape wisdom culture assumes, it will also need a vision for the latent capabilities of young minds. And this vision includes seeing possibilities in those unable, or not yet old enough, to see these possibilities in themselves. By re-visioning schools, and leading them toward a wisdom culture, education asserts its proper status as a template for civilization. Is this too high minded, or fanciful? I do not think so. Reclaiming the ideals of our civilization demands confident, creative action. I make this plea primarily on behalf of the young, yet believe that in serving their core needs we are all elevated, and made non-expendable citizens of a culture of wisdom.

Locating Significance
in the Lives of Boys

*The following is an introductory address to the New York State
Association of Independent Schools Conference in April, 2012
at The Allen-Stevenson School, in New York. The occasion was
the presentation of results from a two-year research project,
supported by The International Boys' School Coalition, on how
and where boys find significance in their lives.*

SOMETIMES SCHOOLS HAVE A MOTTO, and you
often see it on posters — "Education for Life" — and
what a misguided idea that really is. The simple truth is
that education *is* life. Childhood is not a matter of being
a *pre-adult*. It is its own experience and warrants more
careful consideration than it is generally now given. The
first time that you fall in love you don't think to yourself,
"This is a rehearsal for when I really fall in love later on."
You're all in, you want to feel the love, right now, for all
it's worth. That's what students want to feel in school —
and that is the most sensible approach to education, here
in the 21st century.

My research suggests that a key priority for boys is
to have a sense of purpose, and to engage in work — not

labor, but actual work — that reflects their spirit, industry, and desire for urgency. The discovery of one's purpose is, or at least ought to be, a primary reason for going to school. Around the world today, boys — and girls — are aching to know their purpose, and to be needed in *important, visible* ways.

Yet young people can't hope to discover their purpose without first knowing something of who they are, and what they, as individuals, are called to do. This is the essence of what vocation — a calling — means. Educating boys with vocation in mind is, in my view, the most progressive, spiritual, and psychologically relevant action a school can take. Such an initiative is not merely another program, community service project, or extracurricular activity; *it is a living example of how to construct a purposeful life.*

The discovery of purpose is the difference between being paralyzed by life's arbitrariness, and being grounded in a life one can author. Yet because the need for purposeful work is generally unrecognized as a critical source of meaning for young people, it is excluded from a broader conversation about happiness, civility, and community. Of even greater concern, there is virtually no discussion about the meaning of work with young people themselves. Instead, work is confined to the more ephemeral and banal terms of a "job" or "career," which minimize the imagination one might apply to thinking about how he or she might contribute to life on Earth.

What is significant to boys? Or rather, the better question is, when do boys feel significant? I have found that boys will reveal the breadth of what they think when you get right up close, stay patient, and listen deeply. In those moments, boys declare their priorities — what they really want from adults and school. And the answer is evident in their fantasies and stories.

It isn't something that's manufactured or costly, and it doesn't have an "on" button. Instead, it's an attitude, a way of being perceived. Simply stated, it's a desire to be taken seriously, and to live and study in the light of that belief. The subtext of almost everything I've learned in my work and research is that boys want to participate in making the world, and want to be educated by those who believe this is possible.

I believe our collective challenge is to embrace this ancient need, and with a determination that conveys the very seriousness of life. In that embrace is confidence in a child's latent capability: "What I can't do now, I'll learn if you teach me. Show me the way, in a form I can grasp, and I *will* follow you."

We need to do more than articulate this belief, we need to demonstrate it through our own purposeful actions. The outcome should be a new set of coordinates for what it actually means to be well educated. Such an effort points us toward a new understanding that properly relocates education as a guiding force of civilization. Children spend so much time attending to the responsibilities of school, it no longer makes sense to discuss school and growing up as though they were different things. Progressive schools are raising boys as well as teaching them, and I hope you'll raise them to be conscientious citizens.

We've spent too much time following and reacting to half-truths, most of which have been based on the singular idea that the greatest prize of life is upward mobility. It's hard not to be smothered by this idea. I find myself wondering what sort of culture feels compelled to publicly grieve the passing of a techno-genius of digital gadgets like Steve Jobs, and the obvious answer seems to be a culture that recognizes itself as consumers more than citizens. And I wonder if educators who wish to impart the foundations of citizenship in the midst of this confusion have been given an impossibly hard job.

The past decades have taught us much about the brain, and how to teach students. But any vision of education's future must certainly address bigger questions: What should we teach children? And what must they know to find their place in the world?

This is anything but an elitist proposition. It's not fair to allow affluence to hinder one's pursuit of purpose, and the compensation for growing up in poverty should not be an impoverished dialogue about one's prospective purpose. There are no boys for whom significance is insignificant. They just don't know how to tell us. It's our move. With this new awareness in mind, it's time to transcend old arguments about the validity of gender differences, and instead focus upon questions that have traction with students themselves. It is *their* education, and it turns out they have lots to say about what should be included.

A life enlarged by significance is not an accomplishment, it's simply living up to one's promise as a human being. It guides a boy's bond with the world at large, and how to make the world bend, if ever so slightly, to the contours of his ideals. I hope there is still a place in the world, and at school, where those ideals can breathe and assume form.

There are 75 million children in the United States, and two billion worldwide. It seems unthinkable that such a vast group would continue to be the focus of a primarily reductive discourse. A gathering such as this one stands in opposition to that scenario. The interest this study has generated is mostly a measure of how eager we all are for a dialogue that puts our own work in perspective; that shows us that the work of guiding children into the world is as interesting and beautiful as we had always hoped.

What I Learned

This summation of what I learned from dialogue with boys around the world was originally prepared as an address to secondary students at Upper Canada College, in Toronto, November, 2011. The occasion was the tenth anniversary of Upper Canada College's Wernham and West Centre for Learning.

I'VE LEARNED that boys have a lot to say.

I've learned that when boys have a chance to speak their mind, to speak their truth, that they have lots to share.

I've learned that boys like going to boys' schools, except when they don't.

I've learned there is a brotherhood in a boys' school that can last a lifetime.

I've learned there is a bond which can be stronger than blood, but which can be broken by a betrayal of trust.

I've learned that boys like to talk.

I've learned that spoken words are more powerful than written words to most boys. But I've also learned that boys who enjoy writing, enjoy it so much that they can't bear the idea of losing that privilege.

I've learned that creativity is important to boys, until they forget their creative side around age sixteen, when most stop believing creativity is important to their future.

I've learned that boys are desperate for adults to be honest with them, to hear the truth about what they are good at, and also what they are not so good at.

I've learned that boys don't trust people who only give them compliments, and that they don't like people who only give them criticism.

I've learned that boys don't mind giving compliments, if only they could think of one.

I've learned that most boys would love to spend a day with their favorite professional athletes, but that given a choice, a good number would rather hang with Lady Gaga and her crew.

I've learned that boys compete at everything, but usually don't take it too personally.

I've learned that friends are more valuable than anything else a boys has, except *maybe* his family.

I've learned that just about the worst thing a boy can experience is disappointing his parents. I've learned that when boys see disappointment in their parents' eyes they feel like they want to disappear.

I've learned that boys have a lot to get off their chest, and that they're more likely to have a heart to heart talk with their mom than their dad.

I've learned that boys listen closely to what their fathers teach them, and mostly what their fathers talk about is how to be a good man.

I've learned that lots of boys have never used tools, and never had a chance to make something beautiful.

I've learned that mastery of technology is especially important to boys, and that when boys refer to technology, they basically mean computers, because as a society we've come to believe that "technology" means the same thing as "electronic."

I've learned that boys spend about three hours a day checking on Facebook, but actually think Facebook is a huge waste of time.

I've learned that boys would be glad to give up Facebook as long as everybody else is willing to do the same.

I've learned that boys have a lot on their minds, and want a chance to communicate — in a place where they will not be judged.

I've learned that schools are full of leaders, boys who lead by example, who lead with their words, and who lead by serving others.

I've learned that boys want to be recognized for their accomplishments, and that if they are, they will work harder than most people can imagine.

I've learned that effort and work come naturally to boys when it's their idea.

I've learned that boys want to be needed. I've learned that boys want to be taken seriously, and that they want their skills and abilities to be valued.

I've learned that boys often think school is too abstract; that it doesn't have enough to do with real life.

I've learned that the thing boys would most like their schools to teach them more about is social skills.

I've learned that social skills are important to boys because they believe it will help them to meet girls.

I've learned that boys believe one of the best things about growing up is you can have as much sex as you want, and I've learned that lots of boys are pretty nervous about having sex.

I've learned that boys believe the most important thing to teenage girls is big muscles and being athletic, even though a majority of teenage girls say they like boys who talk to them about serious things.

I've learned that animals are unbelievably important to boys, that boys identify with dogs, and love the wildness of big animals.

I've learned that boys like to take care of animals, and would be happier if their schools had animals that casually walked around and socialized with everybody.

I've learned that boys crave dialogue with people who are serious about listening. I've learned that these conversations need to be an ongoing part of boys' lives. I've learned that eight to twelve guys is a perfect size for a good conversation, and that just because a boy does most of the talking doesn't mean he is the most popular.

I've learned that boys want to figure out what they are supposed to do with their lives, and that they want a chance to experiment with those options before they turn twenty.

I've learned that sitting attentively is needed to get into a good university, but is not so good for the spirit of boys.

I've learned that if the head of a school reports to students that there is an emergency downtown, and that volunteers are needed for a rough, dirty job that won't be over until after midnight, and that the job will leave you totally exhausted, almost every boy in the room would gladly volunteer, because boys need to be needed as much as they need friends.

I've learned that boys don't always believe in God, but they do believe in praying, and they do want big questions answered, like how to deal with a death, and how to decide what is moral and immoral.

I've learned that boys like teachers who help them to explore these questions without telling them what to think.

I've learned that every boy has had teachers who he believes have changed his life.

I've learned that boys want to talk about issues, straight-up, no bull, just young men walking their own truth, unafraid to let others hear what they have to say.

I've learned it's awesome to be cool, but maybe not as good as being tall and athletic.

I've learned that when you talk to boys away from classrooms they tend to be more open, and more willing to support one another.

I've learned that living in a city that's just been hit by a vicious earthquake leaves boys stunned, and changes the meaning of what's really important.

I've seen boys cry over the death of a valued friend, and I've learned that when boys express strong emotions, they are often leaders in the eyes of their peers.

I've learned that boys want to write their own story, and that their biggest fear is getting stuck in a job they don't like — a job that makes them feel like someone they are not.

I've learned that boys want to honor their parents by living up to their potential.

I've learned that parents are like an invisible presence in every classroom, and that when boys have to figure out how to handle an important problem, they think of their parents, and it makes the decision clearer.

I've learned that boys will respect me as long as I respect them, and that they take studies like mine very seriously. I've learned that some boys don't want the conversation to end, because talking has opened doors that have been closed for a long time.

I've learned that boys have strong opinions, but can be patient in listening to the opinions of others.

I've learned that boys like the traditions of their schools, but wish they had more say in how those traditions are celebrated.

I've learned that boys want honor in their lives, but don't want to have to engage in combat to get it.

I've learned that boys love theater, would rather learn by looking than reading, have all kinds of heroes, feel like their brains are more tired than their bodies, want to spend more time in the woods, say music is way more important than Facebook, wish their parents knew how hard they worked, believe school will help them to achieve their dreams, and that happiness is more important than grades, winning, status, or power.

I've learned that most boys would prefer to push a heavy rock uphill than write a difficult book report, even though both tasks are of interest.

I've learned that boys' answer to this question tells us that what boys value can only be learned by asking, and that the moment we assume we know what boys think, we stop seeing the truth, and only see what we want to see. I hope I've learned not to do that.

But most of all, I've learned that boys have lots and lots to say, more than can fit in this summary, and more than anybody knows. Except, of course, boys themselves.

Notes

The Purpose of Work

1   Adam Cox, *Locating Significance in the Lives of Boys*, (International Boys' Schools Coalition, New York, 2011).

2   Lisa Wilson, *Ye Heart of a Man*, (Yale, New Haven, 1999) 20–21.

3   Abraham Maslow, *Motivation and Personality*, (1954); quoted in Alain de Botton, *The Pleasures and Sorrows of Work*, (Pantheon, New York, 2009) 113.

4   Michael Lerner, *The Crisis of Values in America: Its Manipulation by the Right and its Invisibility to the Left*, 65–66, in David Batstone Eduardo Mendieta, Editors, *The Good Citizen*, (Routledge, New York, 2001)

5   Robert Rosenthal & Lenore Jacobson, *Pygmalion in the Classroom: Teacher Expectation and Pupils' Intellectual Development*, (Crown House, Connecticut, 2003).

6   Alain de Botton, *The Pleasures and Sorrows of Work*, (Pantheon, New York, 2009) 80.

7   Matthew Crawford, *Shopclass as Soulcraft: An Inquiry Into the Value of Work*, (Penguin, New York, 2009) 11.

8   Simon Hattenstone, *On the Couch with Neutron Jack*, (The Guardian, October 12, 2001).

9   Bob Nelson & Peter Economy, *Managing for Dummies*, (Wiley, New Jersey, 2010).

10 Timothy Ferriss, *The 4-Hour Workweek: Escape 9–5, Live Anywhere, and Join the New Rich*, (Crown, New York, 2007).

Sovereign Minds

1 Milton Friedman, *Capitalism and Freedom*, (University of Chicago, 2002).

On Monstrous Children

1 Alex Williams, *Becoming the Alpha Dog in Your Own Home*, (The New York Times, November 20, 2009).

2 Katie A. McLaughlin, Jennifer Greif Green, Irving Hwang, Nancy A. Sampson, Alan M. Zaslavsky, Ronald C. Kessler, *Intermittent Explosive Disorder in the National Comorbidity Survey Replication Adolescent Supplement*, (Archives of General Psychiatry, Online, July, 2012).

3 Walter Gilliam, *Prekindergarteners Left Behind: Expulsion Rates in State Prekindergarten Systems*, Yale University Child Study Center, 2005).

4 James Flynn, *What is Intelligence?: Beyond the Flynn Effect*, (Cambridge University, 2009).

5 Adam Cox, *Locating Significance in the Lives of Boys*, (International Boys' Schools Coalition, New York, 2011).

Being Harry Potter

1 "B.C. Superhero Sting Results in Child Luring Charges," (CBC News, British Columbia, June 8, 2012).

2 William Deresiewicz, *That is So! That is So!*, (The New Republic, February 22, 2012).

3   Ralph Waldo Emerson, (Journal, April 13, 1834).

4   Wendell Berry, "Living in the Future: The 'Modern' Agricultural Ideal," in *The Unsettling of America*, (Sierra Club Books, 1977).

5   Booker T. Washington, *Signs of Progress Among the Negroes*, (Century Magazine, January 1900).

6   Jennifer Henderson, *Kids A, Adults B–*, (American Scholar, March 22, 2012).

School as Wisdom Culture

1   Susan Sontag, *At the Same Time: The Novelist and Moral Reasoning*, in *At the Same Time: Essays & Speeches*, (Farrar, Strauss & Giroux, New York, 2007) 212.

2   Henry David Thoreau, *Walden*, (Beacon Press, Boston, 1997) 47.

3   *Ibid.* p.21.

Acknowledgments

THE IDEAS IN THIS BOOK evolved slowly over several years, and were enabled by the opportunity to address many school communities. I have been fortunate to visit schools in every region of the United States and Canada, as well as in Australia, New Zealand, South Africa, Singapore, and England. Much of my travel has been sponsored by the International Boys' Schools Coalition. I give heartfelt thanks to the IBSC for their interest in my work, and especially to Brad Adams, IBSC's Executive Director, for his endorsement of my research, and for his intellectual vigor. In the course of completing my research I met many who shared their insights on youth and schools. Among them, I am pleased to acknowledge Gerry Ward, Steve Farley, John Shanahan, Sylvia Menezes, Christopher Post, David Doherty, David Armstrong, John Botti, Marcos Williams, Elaine Williams, Nigel Toy, Brian Lee, Stephen Nokes, Ian Carter, Joe Powers, Ann Clark, Michael Urwin, Andrew Baylis, Paul Tobias, Tim Wright, David Anderson, John Burns, Paul Dudley, Jonathan Hensman, Dirk Wellham, Tim Hawkes, Simon Leese, Roger Moses, Gregor Fountain, Grant Lander, Koh Thiam Seng, Julia Ong, Bernard Teo, Ken Ball, Wayne Parsons, Ron Jury, Ann McLoughlin, Roger Cameron, Warwick Taylor, Rob Long, Margot

Long, Paul Channon, Jim Power, Mary Gauthier, Don Kawasoe, Joseph Cox, Steve Murray, David Trower, Barbara Swanson, Hal Hannaford, Minna Shulman, Greg O'Melia, Jonathan Rosenshine, Stephen Clement, Geoff Roberts, Colin Lowndes, Michael Fellin, Jane Wightman, Kay Atman, Stephen Johnson.

Young people themselves have also helped me to understand my priorities as a psychologist. I've been fortunate to speak with those generous in their insight, and who have been willing to share life's more difficult experiences. I was delighted to find how seriously young people treated these conversations. There was a day in Christchurch, New Zealand when aftershocks of a recent earthquake shook the building in which I was conducting a roundtable conversation with students. In the midst of a discussion about the meaning of honor, several of us momentarily lost our seating, but that didn't stop an extraordinary group of boys from persisting with the topic at hand. That was an instructive moment.

My wife Jacquelyne has, as always, been my most valued reader. My son, Addison, has been patient beyond reason with the time and concentration these writings have consumed. I sincerely hope this work is worthy of both.

A DAM COX is a licensed and board certified clinical psychologist. As a consultant and lecturer on child development, and author of a global school-based research project, he has visited hundreds of schools and organizations in the U.S., Canada, United Kingdom, Australia, New Zealand, Singapore, and South Africa. His books about the emotional and cognitive development of school-age children include *No Mind Left Behind: Understanding and Fostering Executive Control — The Eight Essential Brain Skills Every Child Needs to Thrive* and *Boys of Few Words: Raising Our Sons to Communicate and Connect.* His work has been translated into multiple languages, and his commentary on youth, families, and schools has appeared in many publications, including *The New York Times, The New Atlantis,* and *Newsweek.* In addition to writing and clinical work, he operates a small blueberry farm in Rhode Island with his wife and son.

www.DrAdamCox.com

CPSIA information can be obtained at www.ICGtesting.com
Printed in the USA
LVOW06s1758070114

368463LV00007B/888/P